NATURE

D1742600

NORTHUMBERLAND VILLAGES

Northumberland Villages

GODFREY WATSON

ROBERT HALE · LONDON

© *Godfrey Watson 1976*
First published in Great Britain 1976

ISBN 0 7091 5548 4

Robert Hale & Company
Clerkenwell House,
Clerkenwell Green
London EC1R 0HT

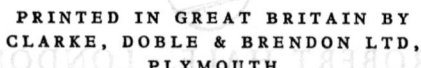

PRINTED IN GREAT BRITAIN BY
CLARKE, DOBLE & BRENDON LTD,
PLYMOUTH

Contents

Illustrations

PICTURE CREDITS

The photographs numbered 1, 16, 17, 18, 23, 32, 34, 38 and 39 are by Hylton Edgar; the others are by the author.

Introduction

When this book was planned, the new 'county' of Tyne-Wear had recently absorbed not only the City and County of Newcastle upon Tyne but also a number of villages in what was previously Northumberland. It seemed a pity to leave them in limbo, as it were, and I have therefore turned a blind eye to the change in boundaries and written of the county as it was.

As for deciding what is, or is not, a village, I have been guided by instinct rather than by any hard and fast criteria. What might rank in a comparatively populous area as a tiny hamlet may well serve as an important centre for a more scattered population. The decision to call a place a village rather than a town is more a matter of atmosphere than anything else and I hope that I have offended nobody by treating as villages one or two places that have often been classed as towns.

Anyone who wants to know more about Northumberland should consult Herbert Honeyman's contribution to the County Book series, which has never been bettered. Then read *The Northumberland Landscape* by Robert Newton and Nancy Ridley's *Portrait of Northumberland*. W. W. Tomlinson's *Comprehensive Guide to Northumberland* has proved the basis for a host of others while the fifteen volumes of the County History supplement Hodgson's *History of Northumberland*, which runs to another seven. For really exquisite sketches of the county, Hugh Thomson's illustrations in *Highways and Byways of Northumberland* take some beating.

These are only a few of the books written about the county since Wallis produced his *Natural History and Antiquities of Northumberland* in 1769 that I myself have found helpful.

I

The Northernmost County

SOMEONE once described Northumberland as a "million acres of fresh air", which was perhaps excusable in view of the facts. For instance it is the fifth largest county in terms of area, yet only the fourteenth in population. When you consider that four-fifths of the latter are squeezed into the south-east corner, and that there is no town in the county proper that can boast more than 15,000 inhabitants, it becomes apparent that there is plenty of fresh air to go round. Then there is the air itself. With nearly a fifth of the land over 1,000 feet and little to stop winds from the north and east from sweeping over the countryside, there is any amount of that. So much so that at harvest time a shrewd east wind does as much to ripen and dry the corn as does any sun with which the county happens to be blessed. The climate, indeed, is not to the liking of everyone. Lord Willoughby de Eresby, for instance, when he was sent north in Elizabethan times to serve as Warden of the East March, complained that "If I were further from the tempestuousness of the Cheviot hills and were once returned from this accursed country whence the sun is so removed, I would not change my homeliest hermitage for the highest palace of all." Admittedly, spring is late and cold and summer cool, often with a sea fret. Yet the back-end (as we call it) can be glorious, with sometimes an Indian summer, and the winter no worse than in many other parts of England. In the higher dales, of course, snow can come deep and frequent, but everyone is prepared for it. At least the climate gives you an appetite!

Rainfall, like everything else climatic or topographical, varies tremendously. The extreme north, say between Berwick and Bamburgh, enjoys 25, and the rest of the coastal strip some 29, inches. Yet near the Cheviots the figure is more like 45 and on the Allendale moors anything up to 60.

It consists of an irregular triangle, this county of ours, and, just as the communications of England are centred on the southeastern corner, that is to say London, so the main roads of Northumberland nearly all lead to Newcastle, which stands in almost the same relation to the rest of the county. From Berwick in the north to Allenheads in the south the extreme length is 71 miles, while the breadth from Tynemouth to Greenhead in the west is 60. Generally speaking, the highest land, which rises to 2,676 feet on Muckle Cheviot, lies to the west, and thence the land slopes irregularly towards a narrow coastal plain.

Apart from the Cheviots, Northumberland is based on the carboniferous rocks, so it is only to be expected that coal should be found all over the place, even on some of the moors. Apart from the main coalfield of the south-east, however, and one or two specific places like Shilbottle and Scremerston, it tends to appear in thin seams which are difficult to mine economically, though sporadic efforts are made, when circumstances warrant it, to reopen on licence the little 'country pits'. More profitable by far is the opencast mining which has been the subject of so much controversy. This consists of quarrying a hundred or more acres at a time, sometimes to a depth of several hundred feet. Eventually the land is restored to agriculture, or some other purpose, but while it goes on, the effect on the landscape is deplorable.

An even older industry is lead-mining, of which a limited amount used to take place just north of the Tyne (as at Fallowfield) but a great deal on the Pennine fells and moors of the Allendales—a bleak and gloomy countryside but also one of rare beauty when the mood takes it. Alas, it is no longer economic to work the lead, and only a limited amount of mining for fluorspar remains.

Such industries as shipbuilding, the production of armaments, electrical equipment and other forms of heavy engineering, are more or less limited to Tyneside, and are therefore outside the scope of this book, as are most of the factories concerned with light engineering that have been set up in recent years to provide work for those displaced by the run-down of coal-mining and the heavier industries. Quarrying still has its place, though the emphasis is now more on roadstone rather than the sandstones from which our buildings used to be constructed, and the grindstones that were once sent all over the world. Nor must we forget forestry and its ancillaries, for this county has proved from the first a happy hunting ground for the Forestry Commission, who have planted much of the moorland peat with huge regimented forests such as Kielder—the biggest man-made affair in Europe.

Among the 'extractive' industries on which the county depends for so much of its bread and butter, an important place must be given to fishing, particularly the catching of salmon and lobsters. The biggest of all, however, is obviously agriculture. The great expanse of hill and moor enables Northumberland to boast the biggest population of sheep of any county in England, except perhaps Devon. The little Cheviot sheep with their long ears and white wool are mostly—and not unexpectedly—to be found all over the north-west of the county while the Scotch Blackface that used once to roam the remainder of the high ground have now to a noticeable extent given way, at any rate south of the Tyne, to the equally hardy Swaledale, which is somewhat longer in the leg —a useful attribute in a countryside where snow is as much a part of the winter scene as the heather and draw-moss that form their staple diet. The development at Fowberry of the Border Leicester by the brothers Culley inspired the production of an improved model in the shape of the Blue-faced, or Hexham, Leicester; and it is these breeds that, when used on hill ewes, produce the cross-breeds known as Half-breds and Mules that graze the lower ground.

Northumberland is not a great dairying county, but there are fine herds of Friesians and Ayrshires; even of Channel Islanders. It is with beef cattle, however, that we are mainly concerned. A generation or so ago it was long odds that any bull you saw was an Angus or Shorthorn, and the white face of the Hereford was unknown. Nowadays there are probably more of the latter to be seen than the Angus and the Charollais (newly imported from France) put together, while the Shorthorn has virtually disappeared. Of the cattle fattening on the lower ground the local crosses and pure-breds graze side by side with great numbers of Irish cattle imported for the purpose. Higher up the hill are to be found the hardy Galloway and, particularly near the Cumberland border, the Blue Grey that is produced by mating the cows with a white Shorthorn bull. We are not much sold on poultry or, indeed, on pigs. The nearest sugar beet factory is too far away for the growing of beet to be economic, and only a modest acreage of potatoes is grown, mostly in the coastal strip; but turnips and swedes are making something of a comeback. So is wheat, while the traditional oats have almost entirely given way to barley.

Economics have, in fact, dictated increasing areas of arable crops. Yet it is as stocksmen that we would wish to be judged— perhaps the best in England.

Three thousand years ago Northumberland, like the rest of England, consisted of one great forest of oak and ash, broken only by expanses of hill and moor and by swamps, of which, now so many of them are drained, we are largely unaware. It had only been a couple of thousand years since man first appeared in the county, probably from the Mediterranean by way of the Irish Sea and through the Tyne Gap from Cumbria. Another millennium had gone by before the people from the continent of Europe whom we know, from their pottery, as the Beaker Folk, arrived; to be followed by another wave from the Continent, who brought with them tools and weapons of bronze rather than stone. The Otadini, as these early Northumbrians were known to the outside world, seem to have been slow in adopting the use of iron, and therefore to have fallen under the influence of the more advanced tribes from what is now Yorkshire. When the Romans arrived on the scene, therefore, they found a people not only of mixed heredity but using a variety of weapons. Nevertheless they met with a warm reception, and it was not until they had built a series of forts stretching from the mouth of the Tyne to the Solway, and linked them with a road that eventually became known as the Stanegate, that they felt secure enough to advance northwards.

To aid this advance, the Romans extended the road (afterwards to be known as Dere Street) that ran from York to Corbridge, up to the Cheviots just east of the Carter Bar, over which the Jedburgh road now runs, and on into Scotland. Subsequently they built the Devil's Causeway from a little way north of Corbridge up to Tweedmouth, and then the Holystone road to connect the two.

When the Romans finally folded their tents and stole away, the Northumbrians—that is to say the Romanized Britons—found themselves with little defence against the Picts and Caledonians, from whom their masters had with varying degrees of success protected them. There began, in fact, an era lasting for a thousand years, when they were always fighting someone or other—or so it must have seemed. Hardly had they beaten off the northern tribes than they became subject to armed reconnaissances, and eventually to the wholesale colonization of the county, by the Angles of North Germany.

These early English settlers seem to have been organized in *ings*—that is to say, in little sub-tribes that consisted of a leader, his immediate family, his relations and hangers-on. Each of these leaders was to build his own *tun* or homestead, consisting at first of a few huts in any *leah*, or clearing, that he could find or hack out of the forest and surround with a stockade. Later, this might develop into a *ham* or village. Often it would be named after the settler himself, so that one finds Ofa's people (the Ovingas) founding the village of Ovingham* and, when it outgrew its surroundings, a fresh homestead of Ovington. An alternative was to call the original clearing after some particular feature, or after the animals, plants or trees, to be found there, and thus to produce such names as Lambley, Birtley and the like.

Eventually the Anglian tribes, having effectually driven out, killed or intermarried with the Weallas, as they called the Britons, coalesced into two small kingdoms, Deira, which began on the Yorkshire Wolds and spread northwards to the Tees, and Bernicia which lay between the Tees and the Forth. It was these two that eventually formed the kingdom of Northumbria which at one time came within an ace of uniting all Britain south of the Forth. It is an intriguing thought that if it had been successful Bamburgh might well have become the capital of a very different England.

With the end of the eighth century came the Viking raids by Norsemen and Danes which started with attacks along the coast and on the unfortunate monks of Tynemouth and Lindisfarne

* Pronounced 'Ovvrinjum'.

(Holy Island), but soon became more numerous and concentrated. Yet they never succeeded in colonizing the county as was the case further south; so that although their influence on our speech has been considerable there are very few Scandinavian placenames to be found.

Probably the most important event in the history of Northumbria for some hundreds of years was the refusal of its kings to accept the suzerainty of Wessex and thus to complete the unification of England. The result was its invasion in 950 by Eadred, King of the English, which led to Northumbria being reduced to an earldom and forcibly annexed. Thenceforward its earls, particularly the Anglo-Danish dynasty that eventually seized power, became a constant thorn in the side of the monarchy; their tacit support of foreign invasion easing considerably the task of William the Bastard when he set out to conquer England, assistance for which he does not seem to have shown much gratitude. His devastation of Yorkshire and South Durham left a vacuum further north* of which Malcolm Canmore was quick to avail himself by invading Northumberland, slaughtering and burning almost at will, and carrying off so many captives that it was said that there was no household in Scotland so poor that it did not own at least one English slave. For a time, indeed, the county actually formed part of Scotland, while for long enough the Scottish kings included Tynedale in their estates, and did homage accordingly. And so there developed a kind of love-hate relationship, triggered off by Northumberland's continuing resentment of southern domination and fostered by the close racial ties between the people on either side of the Border. Indeed, when King John tried to tax the Northumbrians in order to pay for his French wars, they actually volunteered to become part of Scotland; thereby incurring another invasion, this time by the English king.

If the refusal of Northumbria to join Wessex had been the most far-reaching event in the history of the county, it was the accession of Edward I that was to prove the most directly damaging, his attempt to conquer Scotland resulting in a series of wars that lasted for two-and-a-half centuries. In his efforts to hammer the Scots it was inevitable that Northumberland should find itself

---

* Hence the absence of any reference to the northernmost counties in Domesday Book.

the anvil; so much so that, by the time that Elizabeth I came to the throne, a great part of the county was little more than a smoking ruin. Whereas Henry II had been content to instigate the building of the great Border castles to act as focal points in the county's defence against the Scots, it was these Wars of Independence, apparently destined to go on for ever, that dictated the building of the Border towers for lesser men to live in. Originally they formed part of tiny fortresses called peels, which included not only the tower, into the basement of which the most valuable horses and the milking cows could be driven, but a barmkin, or fortified courtyard, to hold the tenants' cattle when attack was imminent. It was these towers that, in the intervals of official warfare, remained the only practical form of defence against the reivers, that is to say the marauding bands of cattle rustlers that the wars had engendered on both sides of the Border. Indeed it was many years after the Union of the Crowns before there appeared in the county any kind of habitation other than the towers of the lairds or the hovels of wattle-and-daub which their tenants could rebuild in an afternoon.

At a time when the gentry of southern England were building unfortified manor houses, and others their cosily thatched cottages, life in Northumberland still remained "poor, nasty, brutish and short", and continued so for another hundred years. That is why one can travel the length and breadth of the county and scarcely find a house (as distinct from a castle or tower, or their derivative) built before 1700.

Styles of architecture vary, of course, with the materials at the builders' disposal, but they are also affected by other influences such as the need for protection from a harsh climate and a rampagious neighbour. The result, so far as Northumberland is concerned, has been the development of a style of building that is rugged, massive and sombre. Not for us the elegance of black-and-white, or of tall Elizabethan chimneys. Not for us the weathered brick or picturesque thatch; nor indeed the Gothic tracery, tall spires and ornate church towers of other counties. You have only to look at the vaulted chancel at Kirknewton, or the church towers of Ancroft or Edlingham, to appreciate how many of our churches had to be built to serve a double purpose, the worship of God and the protection of the parson and his flock from attack—perhaps even the safeguarding of prisoners taken in an unsuccessful raid.

Stone-slab roofs, massive walls, and a general air of weight and solidity, then, are the hallmarks of our indigenous architecture, facts which Vanbrugh well appreciated when he was asked to design Seaton Delaval Hall and the Town Hall of Morpeth. It is very much in this idiom, moreover, that the improving landlords of the eighteenth century built their estate villages to replace the dubious dwellings of the past.

On the whole Northumberland has been lucky in its squires. Most of the big estates still survive, though curtailed by death duties and bowing under a weight of taxation that has made it impossible in many cases to live in the great houses; yet still providing a stable framework for the countryside that is tolerated by most and admired by many. We remain, indeed, very much of a feudal county, rejoicing in enlightened estate management and proud of our resident Duke.

Pits have closed, blacksmiths' shops have disappeared or concentrated on agricultural engineering; other village industries have bowed to the mass-production of the towns; congregations have dwindled, and television has sapped the social life. Yet the villages of Northumberland still serve the purpose that inspired them, namely to provide the focal point of communities perhaps more scattered than in any other county in England. Usually tiny, generally rugged and utilitarian, and often dependent for their chief interest on peel towers or churches, like Oxford marmalade they are perhaps an acquired taste; but that taste once acquired, it remains like the buildings that inspired it, both solid and abiding.

2

The Tyne Valley

WHEN Bonnie Prince Charlie marched south towards Derby in 1745, General Wade was faced with the unenviable task of moving his army across country to Carlisle, in order to cut him off before he could enlist further support. Wade's line of march was by way of Carelgate, the old Carlisle road that meanders down to the Tyne at Newburn, continues by way of what is now a muddy lane along the river as far as Ovingham, then climbs out of the valley towards Corbridge and on to Hexham. It very soon became obvious that he would have his work cut out to move his artillery and baggage train along a track that had never been designed for anything of the sort. The army had no sooner descended Denton Bank than the timber bridge over the burn collapsed under them. Dragging their heavy equipment out of the morass as well as they could, they struggled on to Walbottle Dene, where exactly the same thing happened. By the time the army had reached Hexham it was clear to Wade that he had no hope of achieving his objective, and he returned as best he might. Vowing that never again should an army be faced with such an impossible task, he recommended that a new road be built along the higher ground from Newcastle to Carlisle. And so was born the 'Military', which not only follows almost exactly the line of the Roman Wall but as often as not runs along the top of it, using, of course, the Roman stones as a foundation. Later still, another route—the Low Road—was opened up, departing from the Military road some seven miles from Newcastle, picking up the old Carelgate just before Corbridge, and running through Hexham and Haydon Bridge to rejoin the other at Greenhead.

Where the two roads originally diverge lies the village of Heddon-on-the-Wall. Here one shakes off the dust of Tyneside, and incidentally of the new county of Tyne-Wear, and reaches open country at last. Or almost. It is only a few years ago that the village with its few old houses, its two blacksmiths' shops, its Towne Gate and grand old church, really *was* a village, if only a small one, which was made all the more attractive by the presence of the three hundred yards of Roman Wall that greet you on entering it. It is no good blinking the fact, however, that Heddon, on the Heather Dun or Hill that gives it its name, can no longer be regarded in the light of an olde-worlde village but must be seen as the dormitory for Newcastle which it has virtually become. The old part remains much as always, except that what was once a carpenter's shop has adapted itself to its changed circumstances by selling antiques. Yet by far the greater part of the inhabitants are those who live in the attractive houses and bungalows lining the slopes that overlook the Tyne—and very pleasant homes they are.

But bricks and mortar are not everything: villages are people and, alas, the community spirit of Heddon seems almost to have disappeared. The Women's Institute, of course, still flourishes; Age Concern does its best; but the new and changing population has not yet found its communal feet. Even the Flower Show, last relic of the village life, is in danger of expiring. Yet who knows? With its historical associations, its old church and village pub, perhaps it is not too late.

As you enter Heddon from Newcastle, the first you see of it is Frenchmen's Row, the line of houses, once known as Heddon Square, that was built by Messrs Bell and Brown to house the pitmen who worked their collieries in Throckley. Before they were completed, the rush of fugitives from the French Revolution had begun, and for the next six years they sheltered emigré priests, who erected the big sundial still to be seen there, as a token of gratitude. One of the houses later became the 'Frenchmen's Arms'.

It is the church of St Philip and St James that remains the chief glory of the village. Perched on its little knowe like a Norman castle, it stands four-square to the elements as it has for a thousand years, for there are still to be found traces in it of tenth-century work. It is well worth a visit, if only to see the glorious vaulted chancel and the dogtooth Norman arch that looks as if some medieval giant (or saint) has sat on it, so that it has bowed in the middle.

Follow the Low Road and it is not long before you pass through the Pasture where Horses were kept, now known as Horsley, or sometimes as Horsley-on-the-Hill, in order to differentiate it from Longhorsley or from Horsley in Redesdale.

I say 'pass through' because in this straggling village the main road narrows and the lorries thundering past provide little temptation to "stand and stare". Unless, therefore, you want to stop at the 'Lion and Lamb', an old hostelry which, without sacrificing its original character, has managed successfully to keep up with the times, you tend to leave Horsley all too rapidly. For the same reason the place with its few undistinguished-looking houses, is probably safe from commuters and weekenders. Yet there are undisclosed delights in Horsley for anyone who cares to look for them. The first is a house, dated 1700, but built in the style of the previous century, where Wesley used to preach, and where his writing desk, with its primitive candle-holder, was once preserved. The second is the Manse, an anonymous little house that adjoins the Congregational church, and for which few people would be prepared to spare a second glance. If only they knew what lies behind that uninviting façade!

In 1662 great numbers of the clergy, accustomed to the religious atmosphere of the Protectorate, and terrified at any idea of returning to the fripperies of Archbishop Laud, left the Church of England rather than accede to the Act of Uniformity. Among those who were actually ejected for their views was Thomas Trewrant, the Vicar of Ovingham. The law forbade Nonconformists to meet within five miles of a parish church, but Thomas was nevertheless anxious to find a meeting place nearby, where those of his parishioners who felt as he did could worship. At what was then the west end of Horsley, and only a couple of miles from his old church, he lit upon a cottage whose steep thatched roof concealed extensive attics. Here the faithful assembled, with the farmers bringing their sheep-dogs so that if they were surprised they could excuse themselves by saying that they had met to collect and exchange their straying sheep. At the west end of the cottage was (and is) a tiny window that lit the attic and also served as a lookout over the valley below. Here these devoted men and their families, with little money and in face of the direst penalties, met until the law was relaxed and they could erect, in 1680, their church next door. With its historic associations it is unfortunate that it was found necessary to rebuild the church towards the end of the last century, the money for its upkeep being guaranteed by the rent of a small farm which, because of its Nonconformist associations, came to be known as The Whiggs. The Manse, however, lives on, without its original thatch, but otherwise much as ever. It is not long, indeed, since the lady who lives there discovered to her great joy, and to that of all antiquarians, that the plaster of the house hid behind it the original wattle-and-daub (or, as we would put it in Northumberland, rice-and-gloor) of the fourteenth century. There, behind a glass panel in the entrance hall, can be seen the vertical branches, holed to allow for half-inch horizontals to pass through; into these, in turn, is plaited the brushwood, still with some of the leaves upon it. And there between the twigs is the dried-out mud of six hundred years ago.

For two hundred years after Thomas Trewrant's death the communion set that he had used disappeared from sight. It was not until the roof of the manse was being replaced that it was discovered, plastered up in the wall of the attic where Thomas had presumably hidden it and forgotten to tell anyone. It consists (rather pathetically) of two pewter plates and a battered pewter mug—all that the faithful could afford.

With Ovingham—the Village that Ofa's People created on the banks of the Tyne—we are back in commuter-land once more. Villages such as this come in two kinds; those where old houses have been converted, and those where building estates have been added on. Ovingham, like Heddon-on-the-Wall, is one of the latter but, unlike Heddon, the older part is big enough to dictate how the life of the village should develop.

Most of the new houses lie on the road that descends from Horsley to the Tyne, but there are also earlier developments at the east end. It is in the centre and towards the west that the essential Ovingham is to be found, with its narrow street twisting between high walls, along which you take your life in your hands, for there are no pavements.

Dominating everything is the fine old church of St Mary, with its plain Saxon tower, its long lancet windows and noble chancel. Most of it dates back to the thirteenth century. Opposite, and hidden away behind its high wall, crouches what, for my money, is the gem of the whole place—the vicarage. Its east end belongs to the late fourteenth century, when the house was built to accommodate not only the vicar but three Augustinian canons from Hexham Priory as well. The rest is mainly seventeenth century, and the whole forms an 'L' with a long wing, now used as a parish hall, running towards the street. With its garden descending to the river, its antiquity and its general air of peace and seclusion, Ovingham vicarage is almost in a class of its own. So, at any rate, thought Canon Greenwell, the great antiquary, when he had the pleasure of living there. And so, I dare say, did Thomas Trewrant before he was forced to leave the place.

Before *him* there lived here that Master of Ovingham who proved such a thorn in the side of Henry VIII's commissioners when they came to Hexham to suppress the priory. A firm believer in the Church Militant, the Master confronted them standing on the priory walls, dressed in full armour and with an arrow bent to his bow, urging on the canons in the most uncanonical terms to defend the place to the last man.

All in all, Ovingham, or at any rate the older part of it, has a fascination very much of its own. Despite the fact that the old stepping-stones have now given way to a modern bridge, the place still seems to identify itself with the Tyne almost as a fishing village does with the sea. All the more so because of the way in which the village conveys in its quieter moments the impression of being cut off from the modern world.

Above all there is the almost physical presence of Thomas Bewick, the great engraver. Born in 1753 at Cherryburn, on the other side of the river, his ghost still seems to haunt the village where he obtained such education as he had. It is fitting indeed that it is in the church porch that there now rests a stone that was previously fixed to the west wall of the tower, stating that he is buried here. As a boy Bewick was forced, for want of paper, to chalk his sketches of the animal kingdom not only on the gravestones but on the flags of this very porch. It was in the belfry of St Mary's, moreover, that he and his companions were shut up as a punishment for their sins, and amused themselves by pulling each other up on the bell ropes, until one of them suffered a fall that was nearly fatal. And it was in the vicarage, where the parson conducted a school, that he earned those same punishments.

Altogether, one may be forgiven a pang of regret on leaving Ovingham, on the way to its daughter village of Ovington—the Homestead that the Ovingas founded when they had outgrown the original. As you drive across what was not so many years ago a ford, past the old packhorse bridge and the charming little stone-roofed cottage that faces it, it is difficult to avoid the feeling that you are leaving behind you something left over from the eighteenth century.

Ovington itself is a reminder that we are still in the 'stock-broker belt'. Though council houses now adorn the west end, there are signs everywhere that the commuters and the week-enders are beginning to move in. Extensions, modern windows and general improvement are the order of the day. Even the High-lander Inn gallantly adapts itself to the changing conditions of life, and produces excellent food in modernized surroundings.

In point of fact this is the village's second or third metamorphosis. Through it runs the old Carelgate that proved the downfall of General Wade. In earlier days, therefore, Ovington must have been quite a hive of activity. When the new roads were made to Carlisle, however, the village became something of a backwater, except for the Scottish drovers who, coming that way to avoid the turnpikes, gave the inn its name.

Later still, when the railways killed the droving industry, the place suffered for some obscure reason the indignity of a kind of shanty town of little wooden bungalows growing up at its northern end. This, in turn, has been swept away and has been replaced by a caravan site. How long the social life of the village will survive these latest face-lifts is something that remains to be seen.

From Ovingham westward there runs along the wooded bank of the Tyne a little twisting road where on fine evenings the cars congregate so that their drivers may enjoy the scenic delights, and their children 'plodge' in the river and search for non-existent tiddlers. Until one reaches Bywell Bridge, where the natural inclination is to cross the river and make for Riding Mill. Nothing could be more foolish, for it would mean missing the village of Bywell, a place unique in Northumberland, and perhaps anywhere. In point of fact it is not a village at all, consisting as it does of a castle, a hall, a house that was once the White Horse Inn, an estate cottage or two, a most desirable vicarage, and *two* great churches. Nothing else. It seems likely that this delightful spot was appreciated by the earliest inhabitants of the county, but it was the Romans who were the first to leave an imprint on it in the shape of a bridge over the Tyne. They were followed by the Angles, who christened it after the Spring that they found by the Bight, or Bend, and made it the meeting place of two important estates that ran both north and (more particularly) south, of the river. At the Norman Conquest these became baronies, the more easterly being awarded to Guy de Baliol, the other to Walter de Bolbec.

One's first impression of Bywell is of the magnificent trees, particularly the beeches; but it was the oaks that attracted workers of iron to the place. According to a report made to Elizabeth I, their trade was "all in iron work for the horsemen and Borderers of that country, as in making bits, stirrups, buckles and such others". A hundred years later most of the reivers of Tynedale, who had previously made the lives of the villagers such a torment, had beaten their swords into ploughshares; but Lord Chief Justice North still found that the tenants of the two baronies insisted on escorting him through their territory. "His Lordship was very pleased with their discourse," wrote his brother, "for they were great antiquaries in their own bounds."

It was the family of Baliol, with their vast estates stretching from Bailleul in Poitou all the way up to Scotland, who built the original castle at Bywell, gave Scotland a king and Oxford a college, and then died out. And it was one of the Nevilles, Earls of Westmorland, who rebuilt in the fifteenth century the castle that still graces the east end of the village. Built of Roman stone, part of which, at least, presumably came from the bridge, all that remains is the gatehouse, which was also used as a keep. With its noble battlements, vaulted chambers and spiral stair, however, it is still very well worth looking at, remembering always that, though uninhabited, there adjoins the castle a house that has taken its name.

Between it and the churches there stands an innocent-looking paddock distinguished only by a charming little market cross that gives the show away. For there stood the medieval village, and what stories this paddock could tell; what rusty bits and buckles must lie beneath the turf!

In the curve of the river stand the splendid churches that served the two different baronies. To the east lies that of St Peter, founded in Saxon times, and later entrusted to the Benedictine monks of Durham. Hence its bearing to this day the title of the Black, that is to say, the Benedictine, Church. Parts of it date back to the early eleventh century, while the beautiful high chancel, with its lancet windows, is some two hundred years younger.

A stone's throw away stands St Andrew's, the White Church, originally founded in the seventh century, once the property of the White Canons of Blanchland, and boasting the finest Saxon tower in the county. The rest is mainly thirteenth century, but considerably restored. Behind it lie the sweeping lawns and massive trees that adorn Bywell Hall, built by a branch of the Fenwick family in 1760, but now owned by the Beaumonts, Viscounts Allendale. It was in the great flood of 1761 which swept away the old bridge of Newcastle that the whole village of Bywell virtually disappeared under the waters of the Tyne, which rose to a height of eight feet in the dining-room of the Hall. The garden walls collapsed and all seemed lost, including the valuable stud of horses in the stables. Ten houses were completely swept away and six people drowned. Not so the horses (presumably being more valuable), which were driven into the White Church, where they passed the time by gnawing at the pews, one mare actually taking refuge on the altar.

St Andrew's Vicarage was demolished in 1852, but that of St Peter survives to supply the finishing touch to the idyll of Bywell. Tucked away in a secluded corner, it can have changed little since it was built in the late seventeenth century, with its mullioned windows in the gable ends, and the scroll work that is such a feature of Northumberland houses built about that time.

Up the steep hill, past Bywell home farm, which boasts one of the best-known Aberdeen Angus herds in the country, and crossing once more the old Carelgate as it climbs up from Ovington, you come upon the Low Road on its way to Corbridge, and a little to the west, a narrow, wriggly lane that leads up to the village of Newton, clinging to the side of a hill. Already known as the New Town in 1346, it has for long enough included in its midst an agricultural engineers' business which, in an earlier incarnation, achieved fame among north-country farms for the durability of its 'reapers', as Northumbrians insist on calling their mowers. There is also a prosperous-looking pub in the shape of the 'Duke of Wellington'.

It would be a pleasure to pause at Corbridge and enlarge on a place which boasts a Saxon church, two peel towers, an old bridge and one of the finest Roman forts ever to be excavated. With its two hospitals, its numerous shops and a population bordering on the 3,000 mark, however, one must reluctantly call the place a town and pass on to that Jekyll-and-Hyde of villages once known as At the Oaks, but now as Acomb.

The steep north face of the valley on which the place stands rises from some 150 feet above sea level at Hexham to a height of 700 feet on Fallowfield Fell. Here, bordering the Military Road, are to be found the golden whins that gave Fallowfield its name of the Yellow Expanse, and here are to be seen the remains of the old lead mines and the collieries that have smelted the ore since Roman times, but now at last lie idle.

Now, although the gorse still blooms on Fallowfield Fell, the houses in Acomb, where once the miners lived, are occupied by people working in nearby Hexham, perhaps in the factories that have done so much to restore the fortunes of that ancient town. The rest of Acomb proper is a mixture of rather dull houses both ancient and modern, lining the road to Wall. But take a turning in the middle of the place, signposted Acomb Village, and you enter a fresh world, and one where time seems almost to have stood still. There is no church here, for it is only a short walk along a bridle path to that of St John Lee, which stands on the site of the oratory that St Wilfrid erected in the seventh century.

If the church is some little distance away, everything else that makes a village is here, and how inviting it all is! The focal point of the place is a village square in the centre of which stands a stone 'pant'—that is to say a drinking fountain. On one side are a number of houses dating back, like so much of the village, to about 1750, and including the old blacksmith's shop, now a cow-byre that opens directly on to the square. On the north stands an attractive manor house known as Acomb High House, and on the east and south stand Acomb House and its attendant buildings. The date of the present house is 1736 but some of it is Jacobean, while the weathered brickwork of the garden wall and of the entrance to the grounds is more ancient still. Traditionally North-umbrians have always built in stone. The Romans used to make a thin brick, rather like a tile; but after they retired from the scene no bricks were in evidence until their importation from Flanders began in the fourteenth century, and even then there was little point in using them where the natural product was so plentiful. Perhaps the Acomb bricks came in to the Tyne as ballast; perhaps they were imported especially for the job. Whatever the reason, here they are, and very nice too.

Behind the house stand some of the most ancient farmbuildings in the county, with their Roman stones, and the byre still boast-ing the old cow-ties (or at any rate the roughly dressed poles on which they slid) together with the 'quilled' floor of little pebbles so arranged as to guide the liquids out of the door and into the foldyard.

It is difficult not to appear over-enthusiastic about Acomb village, for here one feels so clearly in the presence of the past—Roman, Anglian, Tudor, Georgian—yet conscious of a continuity which has caused the place to suffer change while never losing its character. Nor, despite a few houses being converted as second homes, has it lost its social life. The British Legion, the Women's Institute, and that institution beloved of Northumbrian villages, the Leek Club, which offers what appear fantastic prizes for the fattest leeks that ingenuity can produce, all survive.

When the Romans inaugurated the Dark Ages by withdrawing their troops from Britain and leaving the Romanized Celts to fend for themselves, the latter were forced to build fresh hill forts in which they could feel reasonably safe if attacked, or to repair those that already existed. One place of obvious strategic import-ance to them was what we now know as Warden Law, a hill which not only dominates the meeting place of the North and South Tynes but also the Roman road which we now know as the Stane-gate. Here they built a settlement fully two acres in extent and defended it, as their masters had taught them, with a rampart of rough stone from the Prudham quarries nearby. Years later, the Angles made their appearance and, no doubt after a bloody struggle, chased the Britons from their stronghold and, hacking down the forest below created their own settlement on the pleasant haughs of Waters Meet. The remains of the original village they retained as a lookout place, and named their new one after it, the Weard Dun, or Watch Hill.

For long enough the only approach to Warden from the south was by boat across the North Tyne, and a pleasant little pub, known as the Boatside Inn, still stands on the village side of the river to prove it. Of all the songs of Northumberland one of the most delightful is "The Water of Tyne", and it may well be that it was here that the hero of the song asked

Oh where is the boatman? I'd give any money,
And you for your trouble rewarded shall be,
To ferry me over the Tyne to me Hinney,
And scull her across that rough river to me.

It was not until the present century that the ferry was replaced by a bridge that bears the inscription "Erected by the Northumberland County Council, His Grace the Duke of Northumberland Chairman ... 1902".

If you cross it, from the direction of Hexham and, turning left, follow the South Tyne for a mile or so along the pleasant wooded road, you may be startled to find a paper mill standing there in all its nakedness, complete with the mountains of waste-paper that are required to feed it. On the other hand, if you carry straight on you will encounter a splendid avenue through which it is possible to catch a glimpse of Warden church, a building of delightful simplicity which, though it was considerably restored in 1765, still boasts a Saxon tower.

On your left rises the wooded mound, known as the Mott, on which the next lot of settlers, the Normans, may very well have built one of their wooden castles. On the right is a cul-de-sac which terminates in a house that once belonged to the Leadbitters. In the early days of the eighteenth century the statute prohibiting Catholics from owning a horse worth more than five pounds was strictly enforced. As might be imagined, among the Northumbrians who so recently had acknoweledged "no other king but Percy", this rule was honoured mainly in the breach. At the time of the Forty-five it fell to the lot of Sir William Middleton of Belsay to impound all the best horses of the Charltons at Hesleyside. In order to avoid a similar fate, the Leadbitter of the day took his most valuable horse, hoisted him into the loft above the stables and surrounded him with trusses of hay and bottles of straw. The bailiffs from Hexham, however, watched the place so carefully that it proved impossible to water him. In the end, the horse became so restive, not to say noisy, that the bailiffs had to be decoyed away while his owner lowered him to the ground, jumped on his back and never drew rein until he had reached the comparative safety of Nafferton.

The road from Warden northwards to Walwick Grange has been known from time immemorial as Homers Lane, not because of any fancied connection with the poet but because of the Hollow Marsh, or perhaps one should say the Marsh in the Hollow, alongside which it runs. Here, in a lonely cottage, an inoffensive chap called Joe the Quilter lived and died, being discovered there one day in 1826 with more than forty wounds. It could only be supposed that, although he was on parish relief, his assailant had hoped to find some money in the house, but as he got clean away no one ever found out. The whole thing was as unfortunate as it was unnecessary, for

> His cot secure, his garden neat,
> He loved the lone and still retreat.
> Glad were his neighbours all to meet
> With honest Joe the Quilter.
>
> Of each he had some good to say,
> Some friendly token to display,
> And few could cheer the winter's day
> Like canny Joe the Quilter.

Britons, Romans, Angles, Normans; all have adapted Warden to suit their own convenience. Now, its character is changing once again. As the meeting point of three estates, the place has until recently consisted mainly of farm buildings and cottages for the estate workers. All that is becoming a thing of the past, however, and its houses and farmsteads have been converted with great skill, and no doubt at considerable expense, into a series of delightful properties in which their owners can find peace after a day's business in Newcastle or Hexham. If villages are people, then Warden is no longer a village, but oh, what a delightful place to live!

Past the Paper Mill, the riverside road leads one to Fourstones. In a document of 1238 its boundaries are described as ". . . from the stone to the second stone and so to the third stone and so to the fourth stone. . . ." The stones in question are traditionally supposed to have been Roman altars. It is noticeable how often that romantic figure, James, Earl of Derwentwater, keeps cropping up in village history, in this case to explain how one of these came to be known as the Fairy Stone. The story goes that one of the secret 'post-boxes' used by the conspirators in the rising of the Fifteen was in a square recess cut into this stone. (Another was in a holly tree at The Linnels, where a bridge crosses the Devil's Water near Dilston). Every evening a boy dressed in green used to steal up to the stone in the twilight, take out the letters intended for the Earl and put his in their place.

It is here, at Fourstones, that one steps for the first time onto the Stanegate that joined together such forts as Corstopitum (Corbridge) and Vindolanda (Chesterholme) before ever Hadrian (and his wall) appeared on the scene. The village itself consists of a pub and two groups of houses, one of them running along the Stanegate and the other clustered round the station. But this is really the poor relation of the next village along the river, in other words Newbrough. Originally the word "burh" signified a fortified place, but by the time that the New Burh appears in history (about 1203) the word had assumed more the meaning that it bears today of a borough or town. Indeed it was not long before Henry III had granted the place a charter to hold a market. No doubt it was always a pleasant spot and Edward I chose to spend a couple of months here on the way north to hammer the Scots and, incidentally, to hot up the 'three hundred years' war' that was eventually to devastate Northumberland.

The most interesting part of the village is the west end, where three large houses stand in their own grounds—Newbrough Hall, Newbrough Park and Newbrough Lodge. There is even a town hall, presented to the village in the last century, which is more

c

than any of its competitors can boast. Close by stands the 'Red Lion', which claims unbroken descent from the twelfth century, but whose chief attraction today lies in the collection of horse-brasses that graces the bar. By the corner of the pub stands one of the boundary stones that gave nearby Fourstones its name. On the whole it is rather a disappointment, for to the uninitiated it looks nothing like a Roman altar, but distressingly akin to a chunk of dark-coloured stone with a flattened top. Inside the Red Lion are to be found, in addition to the horse-brasses, a pleasant aura of rusticity, and grisly tales of a man found murdered in the ancient cellar.

Goodness knows whose idea it was to site the church (dedicated to St Peter) slap in the middle of a Roman fort but, half-a-mile or so further along the Stanegate, that is exactly what they have done, and the surrounding ditch is still clearly to be seen. Near-by is St Mary's Well, whose waters may or may not have once had healing powers, but are now more likely to produce instant typhoid.

After experiencing some years of mild prosperity, when it was augmented by a number of council houses, Newbrough has in the last few decades suffered a number of body blows. Its inhabitants, like those of Fourstones, had for long enough depended for their living on three industries. The local colliery was one and the Prud-ham limestone quarries on nearby Frankham Fell, from which great blocks of building stone used to be sent all over England (and Scotland), were another. The third was the mine at Settling-stones, a couple of miles further along the Stanegate. This part of Northumberland, like the Allendales, is full of curious minerals, many of which are not worth mining. At Settlingstones, however, there has been worked for a number of years a deposit, at a depth of some 150 fathoms, of a crystalline ore known as Witherite, used in the manufacture of soap and cosmetics, and in the refining of sugar.

It was in 1926 that the colliery seams were finally worked out. Then, a few years ago, the quarries virtually stopped production, and now the Settlingstones mine has closed down. A number of the villagers have found work at the Warden paper mill, while the fluorspar mines as far afield as Rookhope, on the borders of Dur-ham, have attracted the mining fraternity. Nevertheless it has not been a happy time for Newbrough, and it is no wonder that many of the inhabitants have had to find work in Hexham or that a few of the houses have fallen into the hands of outsiders.

Westward lies Haydon Bridge, which apparently takes its name from the Valley where Hay was grown—the valley, that it to say of the Cruel Sike, where the medieval village of Haydon once flourished. There would seem to be a number of reasons why one should have developed at the expense of the other. Among them is the Shafto Trust school, that began life in 1685 as a free grammar school and is now a boarding school run by the County Council, concentrating particularly on the preparation of children for a career in agriculture. A more important reason, of course, is the existence of the bridge itself, lately supplemented by a second and much wider one to carry the ever increasing traffic which previously had to wait its turn to cross in single file. The predecessor of the old bridge featured in many a foray run by reivers of both nationalities, so much so that it was normal practice to place chains across it whenever the beacons signalled a raid. In 1528, for example, William Charlton of Shitlington, in North Tyne, together with Archie Dodd and a couple of Scotsmen in the persons of Harry Noble and Robert Armstrong, conceived the idea of running a foray into the domains of the Prince Bishop of Durham. They penetrated as far as the neighbourhood of Wolsingham, in Weardale, where they not only picked up an appreciable quantity of loot but also kidnapped the parson of Muggleswick. On the return journey, however, their luck changed, for on their arrival at Haydon Bridge they found the river in flood and the bridge securely chained. Worse was to follow, for Thomas Errington, the Earl of Northumberland's bailiff, who had been lying in wait, now raised the hue and cry. In the pursuit that followed, the bailiff, to the subsequent astonishment of the warden and his officers, was ably assisted by another William Charlton, "which forwardness in suppressing malifactors hath not been sene afore tyme in Tyndaill men". The reivers were finally overhauled, the laird of Shitlington killed by the bailiff in person, and Armstrong and Dodd caught and executed.

This was an unexpected pleasure for the authorities, whose constant complaint it was that the officials of South Tyne were accustomed to "looking through their fingers" at the reiving that went on. Lord Hunsdon, when he was warden of the Middle March, was to go even further and accuse them of actually aiding the Scots. Messrs Ridley and Heron, he said on one occasion, had taken little or no action to prevent them from burning Haydon Bridge. "I have very vehement suspicions," he went on, "that Ridley himself and some other Englishmen have been acquainted and the drawers of the Scots to Haydon Bridge—which, if I find true, I will make them hop headless, whosoever they be."

But the biggest fillip of all to the lower of the two villages came with the opening in 1836 of the Newcastle to Carlisle railway. "Of the commodious and busy station of the railway," wrote a contemporary historian in a frenzy of ecstatic punctuation, "I can only say, that as my pen approaches the subject, I find it all too elegant. . . ."

With the railway came a paint and varnish works (no longer with us) and a considerable increase in the size of the place, with some pleasant stone houses on either side of the river, a fire station, and finally a new County Technical School. A number of unsightly houses that have lately appeared at the west end have done little to improve the place.

If the village itself is of no great beauty, its inhabitants, at least, have been interesting. The farm of Land Ends, for instance, on the south side of the river, was the birthplace (in 1784) of that excellent painter John Martin, as well as being the home of a friendly bogle, or spirit, known as Josse, who was equally happy to harness the horses while the men were having breakfast as to fill up the hay hecks while they slept.

A contemporary of John Martin was Ned Coulson, also born in 1784, whose feats of walking and running have lost nothing in the telling. On one occasion after walking sixty-five miles to carry out a job, he celebrated his return by competing the same evening in the village sports. If he could find nothing more arduous to do, he would amuse himself by running along the road playing a fiddle behind his back.

Westward again along the Carlisle road there lies on the right-hand side the old Whitechapel Smithy, where the drovers from Scotland used to pause to have their cattle shod before fording the river on their long trek to the fattening pastures of Norfolk. Soon afterwards, a little road to the left drops down to a bridge over the South Tyne, leading to a backwater to which few who have not some particular business there seem to percolate. Those who do not take the turning are missing a lot for, in this angle where the Allen joins the Tyne, there are to be found not only Willimoteswick tower, where the martyred Bishop Ridley was born, but one of the most seductive villages, or rather hamlets, in the county.

In some ways reminiscent more of the Cotswolds than of Northumberland, Beltingham (pronounced of course, like all such names south of Chillingham, with a soft "g") nestles in a wooded corner above the burn that bears its name. You come upon it as a delightful surprise, and if you do so on a summer's afternoon, with a gardener mowing the Manor House lawn and the insects humming in the trees that grace the churchyard next door, you might well wonder whether there is a more tranquil place anywhere.

Part of the fascination, of course, is to be found in the setting, but part in the buildings themselves; pride of place going to this same Georgian manor house with its pillared gates opening onto the village street. All is in keeping; even the school and the outhouses with their stone slab roofs. One house with such a roof is particularly attractive and it looks so old that it comes as quite a shock to read over the door "1907 F.B.L." The initials are those of Francis Bowes Lyon, who was also responsible for restoring— some say over-restoring—the old perpendicular-style church of St Cuthbert. Even the most irreligious could hardly fail to find peace here, or be intrigued by the quaint old carvings on the window arches and the leper's squint through which those allowed to come no further could obtain a view of the altar. In the churchyard stand three enormous yew trees, five hundred years old if they are a day, from which no doubt many a long-bow has been fashioned.

Back to the mainland, as it were, and after Beltingham the deluge, in the shape of Bardon Mill. Named after the Borran, or Barrow, that once surmounted the Hill above it, the place now consists of a few houses of no particular distinction scattered along each side of the Carlisle road, with a pub in the middle and, opposite to it, the woollen mill that has since been converted to the manufacture of drainpipes. Then comes the station and a small

colliery which, like so many of the 'country pits', has now closed
down. A pity, because in such a rural area any alternative employment is an obvious godsend.

Really, Bardon Mill and Henshaw should be considered together,
for they are practically continuous, the former providing the pub
but the latter the church. Once the Wood where Birds sang, Henshaw used to consist of a group of houses on either side of the
main road, but mostly in a clump to the north of it. The fact that
a new and much wider road also passes through it really makes a
nonsense of any village life that may have existed, for the whole
place is now sliced into slivers, leaving the church, with its queer
roof of reddish slate, marooned between the old road and the railway that runs along the riverside. Also isolated is the school that
was once known as the Teem Barns because it was here that
farmers once teemed—that is to say, emptied out—their sacks
of tithe corn, but is now in the process of conversion.

The same fate—that of being sliced through by the new road—
has also befallen the next village—Melkridge. Called after a Ridge
that was noted for the Milkiness of its pastures, this used to be
an attractive little place with a small green. Now it is hardly safe
to cross the road, though perhaps not so risky as it was in the
bad old days when Scottish reivers broke into the house of Robert
Unthank, robbed him of everything he had and shut his daughter
up in a cornbin!

The last village in the county before one finally enters Cumbria is Greenhead. The height from which Green Hill takes its
name is anyone's guess, for to the north and east lies Thirlwall
Common, rising to 800 feet or more, while to the south and west
rises Blenkinsopp Common, a hundred feet higher. Between them
lies the valley of the Tipalt Burn and the village itself, a straggling
place of no great age. To the north of it, however, on a plateau
overlooking the Tipalt, and practically on the line of the Wall
itself, stand the ruins of Thirlwall Castle built, of course, of
Roman stone filched from the Wall, at some time prior to 1300.

Let me now clear up a mystery which must have plagued others
besides myself. Until the last century, the village of Greenhead
can hardly be said to have existed. On the other hand, continual
mention is to be found of a place called Glenwhelt. When the
Angles originally colonized Northumberland, it was into this

corner of the county, and into Cumbria, that a great number of the original inhabitants fled. And here they seem, generally speaking, to have been left in peace, which explains the existence of so many placenames that are British in derivation rather than Anglian, such as Watch Trees, Glendue and Plenmeller, as well as Glenwhelt (the Wild Valley).

The village of that name originally stood on the eastern slope of the Tipalt burn, with a fine coaching inn on the Greenhead side, and it is this inn (once a favourite haunt of Sir Walter Scott, who met his bride at nearby Wardrew) that is all that remains of the old village. Now divided into two houses, it is distinguished by a fine classical doorway, over which is carved a flaming sun and the date 1757, though the Roman bust which once adorned the garden wall has found its way into the grounds of Blenkinsopp Hall. The coach-house, together with the rooms above it, has now been converted into a third dwelling house.

3

South of the Tyne

IT is natural to think of Northumberland as being bounded by three rivers, the Tweed to the north, the Irthing to the west and the Tyne to the south. In actual fact the southern boundary, as will be seen from the map, soon diverges from the Tyne, and it is the Derwent that becomes the southern limit. This divergence begins not far from Wylam, the Village where once there was some kind of 'Wile' (most probably a fish-trap) in the river, along the northern bank of which the older part of the place stretches.

Just as Ovingham is dominated by the memory of Thomas Bewick, so Wylam will always be famous as the birthplace of George Stephenson. Indeed it is well worth while, if you can get someone to direct you, to make the pilgrimage, along the old wagonway that runs below Heddon-on-the-Wall, to High Street House, the cottage where he was born. A pitman who knew him well spoke of George's father as being "as queer as Dick's hatband —went thrice aboot and wadn't tie", and of his mother as "a delicate body an' varry flighty". Yet from this unlikely combination there sprang the genius who, although not strictly speaking the inventor of the locomotive, was indisputably the 'father of the railways'.

At the other end of the village are the houses where dwell Newcastle businessmen; and very attractive they are too, in the shade of the trees that grow so prolifically along this part of the Tyne Valley. Removed from the hustle and bustle of everyday life, they are near enough to the station, which is no great distance from the city itself. On the other side of the bridge over the Tyne and, as its name implies, also secluded among the trees, is Wylam Woods, an Edwardian estate that serves a similar purpose.

The name Prudhoe, the Heugh or Spur of a hill where Pruda (the proud one?) lived, means different things to different people. To some it spells the big I.C.I. factory with its great pile of waste lime left over after the production of nitrates. To others, with its suburb of West Wylam, it is just another pit village. To others again it conjures up a vision of one of the most dramatic of Northumbrian castles. It is in fact all three, and more besides.

We are now, of course, on the south bank of the Tyne, and it is on the bluff overlooking the river that gives the place its name that a gentleman named Odinel de Umfraville built the castle that passed at some time during the thirteenth century to the Percys —Earls, and later Dukes, of Northumberland. With its splendid Norman gatehouse and the keep built in 1173, a pleasant Georgian house within its precincts and the lawns which the Department of the Environment mow with such care, Prudhoe Castle is still a noble sight. It is also a peaceful one, with its wooded dene and little medieval bridge, but it was not always thus. Besieged by William the Lion in 1173, it remained, in the hands of Umfravilles and Percys alike, a bastion against the Scots for many hundreds of years.

Further west along the road towards Hexham lies something very different in the shape of Mickley Square, with its gloomy mixture of Victorian brick houses and modern bungalows, its Social Club and Women's Institute. To the north, however, lies a very pleasanter countryside, alternating between seven hundred and as much as a thousand feet above sea level, across which the Roman Dere Street cuts its diagonal way, and little roads twist and wind from hill to burn and up again. It is a land of windy ridges and open spaces, of dairy farming on the lower ground (even Jerseys are to be seen here), and of beef-cattle and sheep grazing the tops.

The climb itself is both sudden and steep; the road from Mickley Square to the agreeable little hamlet of High Mickley rising five hundred feet in the course of a mile. After which it continues down and up again to another hamlet in the shape of Hedley-onthe-Hill. There are few, if any, signs nowadays of the Heather which covered the original Clearing. The whole place, indeed, seems to have changed, like so many others in this part of the world, with the decrease in the farming population. There remains an unassuming pub, but the chapel has gone out of use. The chief attraction of Hedley, in fact, lies in what one can see from it, for it stands on the western end of a high ridge. Extensive views are a feature of this part of Northumberland, and here is one of the best, extending, as it does on a clear day, westward to the Pennines and north to the Cheviots. It is a sad reflection on its climate that the locals will tell you that "if it is clear enough for you to see Muckle Cheviot it is going to rain, and if you can't it is already raining."

Nowadays there is not much going on in Hedley, but this has not always been the case, for it is not so long since strings of carts used to pass through the village, each bearing its quota of refined lead from the smelt-mill at Dukesfield in Hexhamshire. For here is the Old Lead Road that started at Sparty Lea, in Allendale; then ran past Dukesfield, crossing Dere Street at Leadhill (where the drivers stayed the night) then on past Apperley Dene, through Hedley and Leadgate to Stella, near Blaydon, where the lead was loaded onto ships bound for London.

In a countryside of tiny hamlets it is Whittonstall that assumes the role of a king among beggars, acquiring an importance out of all proportion to its present population, which cannot exceed a couple of hundred at the outside. Ever since the Romans constructed Dere Street, on which their successors built a Tunstall, or Homestead, surrounded by a Quickset hedge, Whittonstall, on its perch seven hundred feet up on a windy ridge midway between Tyne and Derwent, has provided a focal point for this sparsely populated countryside. Once the village could boast a 'full house' of amenities, though why the pub should be called the 'Anchor' is something of a puzzle. But there it is, now undergoing extensive additions, including a dining-room to cater for the growing desire to 'feed out'. There still exist, moreover, a police station, a post office and a general dealer. The school, however, has been converted into a village hall, the Methodist chapel and the blacksmith shop into dwelling houses, the joiner's shop into a garage.

A return to the Tyne Valley also spells a return to the stock-broker belt in general and to Stocksfield in particular. Once the

Open Expanse belonging to the Holy Place—that is to say Hexham Abbey—the village proper consists of the Hall farm, a station on the commuter line, and some neat rows of houses along what is now marked on the map as the Stocksfield burn. It also includes the smart new houses on the Stocksfield Hall Estate and on another known as Guessburn; a name which demands some explanation. It is said that a member of the ordnance survey once asked an inhabitant of the village the name of the burn, to which he replied "Guess!", and as the Guess Burn it solemnly appeared. The place only assumed the status of a village about a hundred years ago, at much the same time, strange to relate, as the remains of the old church were carted away. At that time what is now Stocksfield appeared also as Broomley, Old Ridley and Painshawfield (still shown separately on the ordnance map). It is the latter estate where most of the more expensive houses are situated; while to the east of the village lies its poor relation, Branch End.

Just off the main road stands an old slab-roofed farmstead and a house which bears the inscription "Stocksfield Institute Community Association", and thereby hangs a tale. It must be difficult to preserve or develop the virtues of village life in a locality that has grown up piecemeal from a number of hamlets and building estates. But this is what the inhabitants of Stocksfield have achieved, thereby proving the point once more that it is people rather than buildings that make a village. They have done this largely through the medium of the "Institute and Community Association" with a membership running into four figures. Here the subscribers have been able at little cost to indulge in a variety of activities varying from the Training of Dogs to Old-time Dancing and from a Pre-School Play Group to a Club for 'Senior Citizens'. Harvest Homes, Barn Dances and Village Fairs may have gone the way of all flesh, but here are to be found the modern equivalents.

West of Stocksfield the Tyne valley broadens out on this, the south side of the river, into a series of broad haughs leading to the sprawling village of Riding Mill, with its attendant hamlet of Broomhaugh. The very name of Riding Mill, as in the case of all those places in Northumberland known as The Riding, is apt to cause confusion as to its meaning. In Yorkshire the different Ridings denote thirds of the county: of what is Riding Mill a third?

And the answer is simple, for the former is derived from the Scandinavian *thrithiungr*, while the latter comes from the Old English *ryding*, meaning a place that has been rid of trees; in other words a Clearing. Nor is the Mill very difficult to find, for there it still stands in the main street, tidied up, renovated and converted into flats, but still strongly redolent of the past. Alongside it flows the March Burn, so called because it once formed the boundary between the barony of Baliol and that of Bolbec, which we have now entered. Behind the mill a narrow, curly pack-horse bridge still connects the upper with the lower part of the village.

Most of this upper part consists nowadays of biggish houses standing in their own tree-girt grounds sloping sharply up the valley side. Riding Mill, in fact, has become yet another stud on the stockbroker belt. It still boasts, however, a further reminder of the past in the shape of the Wellington Hotel, once known as the 'Riding House'. Built by one of the Erringtons, in 1660, the place was still in its first youth when it witnessed some of the strange events described in the notorious witch-trials of 1673. It all started with one Ann Armstrong who, finding that accusations of witchcraft against various people in the district were bringing her an enviable notoriety, set herself up as a professional witch-finder. Her dame, she said, had sent her to fetch some eggs from Ann Forster of Stocksfield. However, they could not agree on a price, so they whiled away the time instead by "looking each other's heads"; an activity that appears to have been just as normal among humans as it is now among monkeys, though with less excuse. Subsequently, when bringing the cows in to milk, Ann Armstrong saw, she thought, a ragged old man, who asked where she had been on Friday. When she told him, he said that "the same woman that looked her head should be the first that made a horse of her spirit" and would ride her and turn her into various shapes if only "she would turn to their God". Ann Forster and her fellow witches, he said, would try everything to entice her by riding in empty wooden dishes that had never touched water, and in eggshells, and would show her how to obtain food "by swinging a rope", but that if she did not eat what was provided she would come to no harm. Ann then "fell down dead* and continued dead

---

* In a faint.

till towards 6 that a.m.", since when she had two or three fainting fits every day.

A little before Christmas she was lying in a faint when she saw Ann Forster, who bridled her and rode her astride to meet the coven at the pack-horse bridge at Riding Mill. As soon as her rider dismounted, she resumed her own shape and saw, among the others, "a long black man riding on a bay galloway,* whom they called their protector". After the witches had turned themselves into cats, hares, mice and so forth, apparently just for the fun of it, she was bridled once more and ridden home. All this was repeated on six or seven nights, on the last of which the witches all met at the Riding House, where their protector sat in a gold chair.

On another occasion, on Collop Monday (10th February), Ann Armstrong swore she had been ridden with an enchanted bridle by one Michael Aynsley. At the sabbat to which she was taken, Lucy Thompson confessed to the devil of her particular coven that she had bewitched a horse to death, and also an ox when it was drawing a cart. The devil congratulated her, whereupon the others all piped up with stories of killing a horse in Prudhoe, of causing a child to pine to death, and so forth. Aynsley and a friend of his had done particularly well, for they had bewitched a horse belonging to Mr Errington of Riding Mill, "and they rid behind his man upon the said horse from Newcastle like two bees, and the horse, immediately after he came home, died." Others had played tricks on the miller, making "the stones all grind together till they had flown all in pieces," and so forth.

On a ridge seven hundred feet above sea level, and some miles further up the March burn, stands the village of Slaley. Open to all the winds that blow, this is another of those places south of the Tyne where one can enjoy magnificent views. No longer can the place be described as a Muddy Clearing. Instead, there is an atmosphere of orderliness, respectability and peace in this long, straggling village which even the caravan site at the Townfoot has not spoilt. Church, chapel, two pubs and a number of surprisingly affluent-loking houses stand well back from the road, adding a feeling of space to the village's other virtues. The 'Rose and Crown' looks old. The 'Travellers' Rest' bears over its door the words:

* Pony.

If you go by and thirsty be,
The fault's on you and not on me;
Fixed I am here, and hinder none
To refresh, pay and travel on.

No doubt Slaley's most famous citizen, James Pigg, the huntsman whom Surtees immortalized in "Handley Cross", spent many a happy hour in one or both.

From Slaley one takes the Blanchland road over the moors, crossing the old Lead Road and running past acres of heather and bracken interspersed with shooting butts—for this is a great place for grouse—and notices begging one to "Beware of the Adders". There are signs on both sides of the road of extensions that the Commission is making to Slaley Forest, but by the time that one has dipped down to the Acton burn, with its derelict lead mine close by, and up again onto Blanchland Moor, one is back with the grouse again, the new Derwent Reservoir shining and rippling in the valley to the east.

Blanchland, nestling as it does on the banks of the Derwent, 800 feet above sea level. is not a place to be treated lightly in winter for, because of the steep hills that lead down to it from either side, it is only too easy to become snowbound here. In the height of summer it is almost equally hard to get *into*, for this is one of the showplaces of Northumberland, and indeed there are few prettier villages in England.

It was in 1165 that Walter de Bolbec granted land on the north bank of Derwent to twelve canons of the Premonstratensian order from Croxton in Leicestershire. Here they built an abbey; complete with inner and outer courtyards and gatehouse, its own corn mill on the Shildon burn, and fishponds close by. Later they added a fulling mill and silver refinery, for the lead ore hereabouts was always rich in silver. In memory of the White Glade in Normandy from which the order originated, they called the abbey Blanche Lande.

Since then Blanchland, like Prudhoe, has seen some stirring times. In 1295 its abbot was one of the few ecclesiastics to be summoned to Parliament. Later it became the target of a band of marauding Scots who, losing their way in the mist, would have overshot the place had not the monks, to mark their supposed deliverance, rung the abbey bells. Whereupon the Scots, returning, broke down the gates, murdered a number of the canons, set fire to the buildings, and rode off with what loot they could find.

In 1327 Blanchland was burnt again by the Scots under the Earls of Moray and Douglas, and Edward III made his confession at the abbey before marching north to obtain revenge for their depredations. After the Dissolution, the estate came into the possession of the Radcliffes, afterwards Earls of Derwentwater. About 1623 the Forsters of Bamburgh succeeded them, adapting part of the abbey into a manor house and other buildings into cottages. Some seventy years later Lord Crewe, then Bishop of Durham, married Dorothy Forster, who with her brother Thomas, had inherited both the Bamburgh and Blanchland estates. He paid off the mortgages on both, and left them in trust as a charity. Hence the name, Lord Crewe Arms, given to the inn into which the manor house finally developed. It is well worth a luncheon visit if only to look at the rooms, each bearing a name connected with the Jacobites, for it was Tom Forster the younger who, in 1715, commanded with such conspicuous lack of success the rebels at the battle of Preston, and was subsequently condemned to death. In one of them is a curious chimney-piece which contains a hiding place where Dorothy Forster's niece, the more famous Dorothy, is said to have hidden her brother after she had rescued him from Newgate.

When John Wesley visited Blanchland in 1747, he found it a pretty desolate place, but very soon afterwards Lord Crewe's trustees reconstructed the village for the benefit of the lead-miners who lived there, using much of the material from the ruined abbey, and roofing the houses with the traditional stone slabs. In doing so they produced something which, while very reminiscent of a college quadrangle, has a charm all of its own. At one end is the gatehouse through which one enters the village proper: at the other the old bridge over the Derwent. To the north of the quadrangle stands the abbey church dedicated to St Mary the Virgin, and restored at the same time as the rest of the village. On the chancel floor is the tombstone of one of the abbots, bearing a fine cross, a crosier on one side and a chalice on the other. Another stone commemorates one Robert de Egleston, who must have been one of the abbey foresters, for it is carved with a hunting horn, bow, arrow and sword.

So much for what used to be the barony of Bolbec: now for the villages of what is now known as the Shire. There is only one difficulty. Apart from a single small hamlet, which we shall certainly visit, there aren't any!

The kings of Northumbria had a curious habit, when making individual grants of land, of often including with them many of their sovereign rights. When Queen Etheldrid endowed the newly formed bishopric of Hexham in 674 it was on such terms that she gave Wilfrid lands from her dowry. Subsequently the regality passed to the Bishops of Lindisfarne (Holy Island) and by the twelfth century had found its way into the possession of the Archbishops of York, complete with all the judicial and administrative authority which its previous owners had enjoyed. It was not in fact until a special Act of Parliament was passed in 1572 that Hexhamshire became part of the county of Northumberland, and the king's writ ran once more in that part of the world.

The modern Hexhamshire is now but a pale shadow of its former self, geographically as well as administratively. It runs south of the Tyne to the border with County Durham, east as far as the Devil's Water and west as far as the Allendales. It is a land of moor and fell, of heather and 'white grass', that varies in height from five to fifteen hundred feet; the different moors and 'commons' being divided from each other by little wooded glens. In such a countryside, where one can see for miles, farmsteads, usually protected by plantations from the westerlies that sweep over its ninety-two square miles, stand out in stark isolation.

It was in 634 that Oswald, the Christian king of Northumbria, defeated the heathen Cadwallon and his Britons at the battle of Heavenfield, not far from Chollerton. Cadwallon himself, however, escaped from the carnage and made southward. It was almost certainly on the Rowley burn that Oswald's men overtook and despatched him, and it is about here, on the tongue of land between the Rowley Burn and the Devil's Water, that there now stands the 'capital' of the present Shire, in the shape of Whitley Chapel.

Named after the original Clearing of White Grass, the title differentiating the place from Whitley Castle on the Roman

St Philip and St James, Heddon-on-the-Wall

The packhorse bridge at Ovingham

St Michael's, Warden

Haydon Bridge from the south

Converted houses at Warden

(*top*) The manor house at Beltingham

(*bottom*) Glenwhelt, once a coaching inn

The post
office and
'Lord
Crewe
Arms',
Blanchland

The market square, Allendale Town

Prudhoe Castle

An old-fashioned pub: the 'Fox and Hounds', Whitley Chapel

Underneath Allendale Town: the Blackett Level

The fluorspar mine, Allenheads

Maiden Way, refers to the Chapel of Ease that was erected there as a centre of worship for the Low, Middle and High Quarters of Hexhamshire, but which has functioned since 1764 as a parish church in its own right. From very early times there had been a chapel of sorts here, which had been rebuilt some time before the Restoration as a school. Then competition appeared in the shape of the Quakers who, as a result of George Fox's visits, were to obtain a firm foothold both hereabouts and in East Allendale. The chapel hill became a favourite meeting place for his followers and, in self-defence, "great number out of curiosity resorting to them, the said chapel was made fit and appropriated to divine service" once more. It proved too small for its present purpose, however, and in 1695 subscriptions were raised in order to increase its size. Later the chapel was rebuilt but for some reason was never consecrated. Finally the churchwardens complained to the Archbishop of York that "Some of us being twelve miles from Hexham, which is very hard upon us, especially in the winter season, when the days are short, and the roads is bad, we have to come home in the night, sometimes eleven or twelve o'clock."

A small, plain building, with its walls whitewashed inside, and the Lord's Prayer, the Apostles' Creed and the Ten Commandments inscribed on them, St Helen's compares well with the more ancient churches in the county.

Church, school and church hall, all are here and provide the focal point for an overly scattered population. Once there was a blacksmith's shop as well, and in the churchyard is still to be found a stone "Sacred to the memory of Robert Stoker of Chapelhouse who died 6th September 1832, aged 63 years.

> My anvil and hammers lie declin'd,
> My bellows have quite lost their wind,
> My fire's extinct, my forge decay'd,
> My vices are in the dust all laid,
> My coals are spent, my iron gone,
> My nails are drove, my work is done,
> My mortal part rests near this stone,
> My soul to heaven I hope is gone.

It is not long since Hexham was justly famous for the gloves known as Hexham tans. No doubt the tiny cluster of houses that complete the village of Whitley Chapel once housed men who

D

were connected with their manufacture, for near at hand lie farms such as Okerland, where the ochre was produced, Mollersteads, once noted for the mallows that were also used for dyeing, and Dye House itself. Last but not least is the delightful little white-washed pub, once known as 'Click-em-in' but now as the 'Fox and Hounds'.

4

The Allendales

THIS chapter is concerned with three rivers that flow northwards from the Pennines to join the Tyne—that is to say, with the East and West Allens and the South Tyne before it turns the corner at Haltwhistle. It is perhaps the least-known part of Northumberland, yet one of the most interesting. The Pennines, of course, are chock-full of minerals, the most important of which has always been lead, together with the silver that, in varying proportions, it contains. So old is this industry, now almost defunct, that the wealth it had brought to the British tribes was one of the principal reasons for the Roman invasions of England. Except perhaps in the Dark Ages which followed their retirement from the scene, men have continued to mine ore from the upper reaches of the East and West Allens and to smelt it in furnaces fed with peat, and subsequently with coal, from the valley of the South Tyne.

It is an industry that has dominated this part of Northumberland (and the neighbouring districts of Cumbria and Durham) at least as thoroughly as coal mining has other parts of the county. Perhaps more so, for in such a desolate part of the world as the uplands of the Allendales, the alternatives, (particularly that of profitable farming) are restricted indeed. It is also an industry that, for geological reasons, must often be carried out at anything up to two thousand feet above sea level. The result is a countryside that is now dotted with derelict workings, crumbling stone buildings, occasional chimneys and the openings of the 'levels' along which the ore was brought out of the mines. Not to mention the scars left by 'hushes', in other words the damming up of burns and the subsequent release of the water to wash away the topsoil from the outcrops of ore—a method of mining older even than the Romans. Traditionally, the miners used to supplement their incomes by farming, so that this is also a countryside sprinkled with smallholdings. On a sunny day, particularly one on which the clouds cast their shadows on the fells, the Allendales are picturesque indeed. Let the sun go in, however, and they assume a desolate and gloomy look reminding one of the hardships that the old-time miner so steadfastly endured.

The way from either Hexham or Haydon Bridge is across an expanse of 'white' moorland, where Swaledale sheep graze, peewits wheel and curlews cry; then down again to the Dene where Wildcats once roamed—in other words, Catton. Once the inhabitants —or most of them—earned their living in the lead mines near Allendale Town. Nowadays they travel by bus to Allenheads and Rookhope, where the mining of fluorspar (used for hardening steel) now goes on. Yet the place bears no resemblance to a mining village. Built on both sides of a wide, curving road, in a wooded valley, it consists mainly of a mixture of whitewashed houses (including the Crown Inn) and cottages roofed with the traditional stone slabs. An impression of space is achieved by the grass bank on one side of the road and the front gardens on the other. The school is now a Field Centre for kids to stay and experience the delights of an unspoilt countryside. One of the two chapels is closed, and some of the houses are now occupied by retired people from elsewhere. Otherwise, life in Catton seems to go on much as it has always done. Since it was first mentioned in 1295 the place only seems to have hit the headlines on two occasions. The first was when, inevitably, it was burnt by the Scots. The second was in 1715 when seven Jacobites, including the Reverend Robert Patten, a curate from Allendale who had been appointed chaplain to the general, Thomas Forster, joined the Derwent Valley contingent on the moor here, at a place still known as Rebel Hill. After the surrender at Preston, Patten saved Forster's life by knocking up a pistol that had been levelled at him, saved his own life by turning King's Evidence and then, out of gratitude, wrote his *History of the Great Rebellion*, which is the standard work on the subject of the 'Fifteen'.

At the south end of the village are a number of villas which seem quite out of keeping, until very shortly afterwards there appears the sign that heralds Allendale Town, and you realize that all this is virtually the beginning of a summer resort.

Despite its designation, which only exists, of course, to differentiate it from the valley of the same name, and despite its claim (disputed with Hexham) to be the heart, or centre point, of Great Britain, this is only a decent-sized village. But what a village! At first it looks like nothing more than a seaside town without the sea, and it is not until you sweep down over the bridge and between the trees that the place assumes the appearance more of a kindly village built round a village green.

In the last century Allendale Town was described somewhere as "a neat little town, almost every other building of which is a public house for the miners". Since the lead industry deteriorated, however, their place has been filled—no one seems to know why —by visitors from all over England who want to enjoy an unspoilt countryside, which happens to be criss-crossed with footpaths and rights of way that enable them to walk the surrounding moors, and presumably imbibe the healthful air!

The heart of the village is the considerable market square, which was once the focal point not only of the place itself but of the Allendale valleys and the lead industry in general, where the produce of the little farms was collected and either sold or transported to Hexham. And here, grouped round the square and the buildings that form an island in its midst, stand half-a-dozen hotels that have grown out of the taverns that used to slake the miners' thirst, and the little Hare and Hounds Inn that hardly seems to have changed at all. Other hotels and boarding houses, and a few three-storey buildings, are dotted around the village, interspersed with curious old houses like 'The Pharmacy', a biggish whitewashed building which includes a 'Chemist and Druggest' that looks as if it has stepped straight out of the last century.

In North Northumberland it was the Covenanters, in their flight from persecution—and particularly William Veitch—who were responsible for the spread of Presbyterianism. Here in the Dales it was the Quakers who filled the religious gap created by the paucity of churches in a countryside where long distances and difficult travelling conditions have always been the order of the day. But not for long; for the dales became a favourite hunting ground for John Wesley, whose bright idea it was to preach here when the Pays were held—in other words the half-yearly fair day when the lead miners received the balance of their wages after living on a pittance for the remainder of the time. The measure of his success is still to be seen in the number of little chapels dotted about the district, many of them, alas, now in disuse. In 1884 the records of the Allendale circuit showed no fewer than eleven Wesleyan Methodist and another eleven Primitive Methodist chapels.

In Allendale Town, therefore, it is no surprise to find not only a parish church and Quaker meeting house, but two Methodist chapels as well. Despite this assortment of Christian worship, however, a whiff of the bad old days when fire-worship formed part of our pagan rites still survives. Every New Year's Eve a grand bale fire blazes in the square, round which dance the guizers, with blackened faces and in fancy dress that varies from year to year.

Chosen by a committee, the guizers must have been born and bred in the valley, and there is a waiting list of those anxious to take part in what is a strenuous and sometimes quite dangerous performance. Dangerous because, before lighting the fire, they first parade the boundaries of the village bearing on their heads blazing 'kits'. These are barrels with the ends cut off and filled originally with tar, but nowadays with a mixture of grease, shavings and paraffin. In the darkness of a December night, the whole performance provides an eerie, and to the imaginative almost a satanic scene; and people come many miles to watch the ceremony that has survived some fifteen hundred years.

Spare a moment, as you descend the road known as the Peth towards the delightful old buildings of Bridge End, to walk along a path to the right which follows the river bank. For here, among the gloom of the trees, is to be found the exit of the Blackett Level, a stone-lined tunnel in the cliff face, that apparently leads into the bowels of the very hillside on which the village stands, and out of which issues a stream of water draining an old lead mine. And not only water, for here also are the lines of a wagonway along which ponies used to draw the ore along the riverside to the Allen Smelt Mill.

Back to the road then, and past the five lane-ends of Thornley Gate to the Allen Smelt Mill itself, now used as a depot by a haulage contractor. This was once a pretty considerable place, with two roasting furnaces, five ore hearths, two refining furnaces to separate the silver from the lead, and a reducing furnace. Originally two chimneys carried away the soot and smoke, but the lead fumes proved so poisonous that two flues built of stone, half above and half below ground, were built, connecting with a fresh chimney that still forms a landmark a full three miles to the west.

After Allendale Town the road along the East Allen soon mounts to 1,000, and sometimes to 1,200 feet, through tiny hamlets with names like Dirt Pot and Sparty Lea, and past the equally tiny chapels in between. On either side the dale spreads out in the chequer-board pattern of little stone-walled fields and small farmsteads so typical of the Allendales. Here the miners and their successors have for generations milked a few cows and raised what stock they could on the limestone that brought them health but little sustenance. Now, alas, the buildings of many of these smallholdings, incapable as they are of supporting a family without any other means of livelihood, are untenanted and mouldering away. What cows are still milked are no longer the Dales Shorthorns for which the valleys were once famous, but the higher-yielding black-and-white Friesians. To the west can be seen the old Carrier Way along which the strings of pack ponies used to carry the ore over the moors from the mines below Killhope Law on its way to the Allen Mill: to the east the Black Way and the Broad Way wriggle their way upwards towards Dukesfield, in the Shire.

A greater concentration of little farmsteads and the presence of a 'low' road running parallel to the main one, such as it is, mark the beginning of the descent to Allenheads in its wooded hollow. Here is another astonishing village, perhaps even odder than Allendale Town. Above it stretch the moors that provide some of the finest grouse-shooting in England, two hundred brace in a day being quite a common bag. Then come the ski-slopes lately discovered in the search for do-it-yourself winter sports. There is no ski-lift, but a ski-tow, and down below in the middle of the village is the pleasant tree-girt Allenheads Hotel which provides the headquarters of the Northumberland and British Norwegian Skiing Association. All this should have revived the fortunes of a village that originally only existed because of the lead mines. Unfortunately, with the natural cussedness of the weather, the bitter winters that in the past have regularly cut Allenheads off from the outside world have failed for the last few years to produce enough snow, and the fortunes of Allenheads are once more threatened.

Right slap in the middle of a village that remains a strange conglomeration of old buildings, barns and stables once connected with the lead industry, and surrounded by the terraced houses of the miners that worked in it, is the old washing floor extending for an acre or more, where hordes of women and boys once washed one-seventh of all Britain's lead ore. Now it has become the yard surrounding the shaft of the British Steel Corporation's mine, where fluorspar—and possibly fresh seams of lead—are being sought.

The inhabitants of the place are traditionally 'chapel'. The alternative until lately would be to attend "Lord Allendale's Private Church"; Lord Allendale, a descendant of "the richest commoner in England" and as a Beaumont, the inheritor of all the Blackett property in the Allendales, being the Lord of the Manor. Now, alas, it has fallen into disuse, but there it still stands, an example, if ever there was one, that there are more ways than one of approaching a church. Here it can entail an astonishing walk through the fir woods that line the hill above the village, threading one's way between old mine shafts and skipping over the water that still seeps from the workings.

Allenheads is little more than a mile from the Durham border, from which, at a height of 1,700 feet, there stretch before one in all their majesty the fells not only of Durham but of Cumberland, Westmorland and the North Riding as well, for it is hereabouts that five counties nearly met. Six or seven miles in the direction of Alston and one can turn back along the Coalcleugh road that leads down the West Allen, and quite soon be in Carr Shield. It is sad to pass, without even realizing it, through Coalcleugh, known for so long as the highest village in England but now consisting only of a few deserted buildings that have died with the lead mines that bore them.

Carr Shield was once Carrisideshield—the Summer Hut on the Rocky Slope—and it is not a bad description, for it stands on a terrace above the West Allen. At a mere 1,300 feet we have now left the bleakest and wildest part of the valley, and are heading for civilization once more. In this part of the world anything more than half-a-dozen houses and a church, chapel or pub constitutes a village; and Carr Shield certainly qualifies, though one has nearly passed through it before the fact becomes apparent. The first signs are a splendid avenue of trees which comes as a pleasant surprise after the bleakness of the moors; then a dozen houses straggling at intervals along the road, a tiny post office and a Primitive Methodist chapel. Then the parsonage, and opposite it a fine school built by the Beaumonts in the last century and reported to be the highest in England, and finally a little church, now disused.

Ninebanks has borne that name since 1228 at least, and probably for long before that, and its derivation is not far to seek, for a Northumbrian always calls a hill a bank. What is not so easy is to decide which are the Nine Hills in question. Built on two shelves above the river, its southern end, consisting mainly of the church and vicarage, stands higher up than the rest of the village (such as it is) which lies some half-a-mile down river. Here are a dozen houses, a farm whose hemmels* open directly onto the street, and a modern building entitled Manor House. It is the latter's predecessor, however, that provides the chief interest in Ninebanks, in the shape of an old tower attached to one of the houses on the other side of the road. In fact this is the remains of what must have been more than a peel tower; almost a miniature castle, the arms it used to bear being those of Sir Thomas Dacre, who governed Hexhamshire in the time of Henry VIII.

Just after Whitfield Hall, and before one reaches the junction of the West with the East Allen, a little road climbs out of the lovely wooded valley on to the moors once more, and down again to the South Tyne. One might be forgiven for describing this valley as 'neither owt nor something'—or perhaps both—for at one moment one is driving along the haughs bordering the river; at another over moorland a thousand feet above sea level, then descending to the river again, and so on, travelling ever southwards. It is a countryside of stone walls, and its roads, such as they

* Partly covered cattle-yards.

are, provide a number of hazards in the shape of loose stones knocked off the walls, as well as of straying sheep, sharp corners and little sudden hills. That one is now very close to Cumbria is evident not only from the view of its fells covered in a blue haze but by the sight of men up ladders whitewashing the houses.

Sandwiched between road and river, where once grew a Wood belonging to Collan, the Provost of Hexhamshire, lies the tiny hamlet that bears his name. For long enough Coanwood housed the miners who worked the little colliery nearby. Now, like so many others outside the main coalfield, the pit has closed down, the Methodist chapel lies derelict and the pitmen work elsewhere.

Knarsdale, Knaresdale; some maps spell it one way, some another, but it takes its name from the valley of the Knar Burn which, in turn is called after a Rugged Rock, and the inhabitants know it as Knarsdale, so that is that. It can hardly be called a village in the usual sense of the word; yet it includes a 'hall', a church and a pub. Indeed it is a queer kind of place, which looks as if some giant had walked up the valley dropping its different elements at intervals as he went. First one encounters the Hall, a delightful seventeenth-century farmhouse of rough-hewn stone, complete with stone-slab roof and mullioned windows. It bears all the signs of having been built on the motte or mound of a Norman motte-and-bailey castle, and there are even traces of a moat. Nearly half-a-mile further on appears a little church, followed in turn by the 'Kirkstyle Inn and Sportsmen's Rest', now undergoing considerable improvement. Then a farm, a house or two, another farm, another house or two strung out along the road, and finally Stone House Farm with its roof of thick Alston slates and stone-roofed buildings, followed by some half-dozen more houses dignified by the name of Knarsdale Town Green.

In the churchyard there used to stand a gravestone—for all I know it may be there still, though I haven't been able to find it—commemorating one Robert Baxter who expired on 4th October 1796, from eating a piece of bread and butter he found when climbing the fell to count his sheep. He died convinced that it had been poisoned by a neighbour with whom he had had a violent quarrel, a conviction apparently shared by others, for the inscription read:

All you that please these lines to read,
It will cause a tender heart to bleed;
I murdered was upon the fell,
And by the man I know full well,
By bread and butter which he'd laid,
I being harmless, was betrayed.
I hope he will rewarded be,
That laid that poison there for me.

Do not be deceived by Slaggyford's unprepossessing name, which only refers to the Muddy Ford over the Knar Burn, in the fork of which the village nestles. It is overshadowed to the east by Williamston Fell, with its neighbour Kitten Tom, and to the west by Black Hill, each rising to more than 1,500 feet. It was in the bad old days, in the reign of Elizabeth I, that those arch-scoundrels, the Armstrongs of Whithaugh (in Liddesdale) ran a foray against Kirkhaugh, a little further up the valley, and were pursued by the indignant inhabitants. The Armstrongs, who were, of course, slowed down by the cattle they had lifted, saw them coming, however; laid an ambush and captured the lot, adding insult to injury by extorting a ransom of £180.

Slaggyford itself consists of a couple of dozen houses and farms, many of them (including the post office) with the traditional stone-slab roofs. Perhaps it is the result of hard times in hill farming; perhaps because the Pennine Way, which here follows the line of the Romans' Maiden Way, brings walkers along the valley; perhaps because the place is so near to Cumbria where such goings-on are comparatively common, that this has become a 'bed and breakfast' village, as indeed to some extent has Knarsdale. One such hostelry is brand-new, built of variegated stone and entitled, rather surprisingly, 'Crianlarich, Peace and Plenty'. Another, the entrance to which is graced by a cart drawn by a plaster horse of gargoyle mien, appears as 'The Island, Bed and Breakfast'. Opposite stands Broad Mea Farm, in the yard of which stands what at first looks like the lower floors of a peel tower complete with arrow slits, but which, on closer acquaintance, turns out to be a re-roofed stone barn with ventilation slits, bearing the date 1791.

So much for the east side of the river. By retracing one's steps it is possible to cross to the other side and come upon Lambley, an incredible little place that takes its name from the haughs a little further north, originally known as the Pastures where Lambs were kept. Like Coanwood, the place once housed the miners from a small colliery nearby. You enter the village down a narrow street, which winds its way past the church to a little humpty-back bridge over a disused colliery line which once linked up with the railway from Haltwhistle to Alston. Not far away there rises, 110 feet above the level of the river, the viaduct that carries that same railway over the South Tyne. This is a valley that in winter can all too easily become impassable to motor traffic, so that one cannot help sympathizing with the South Tyners in their efforts to preserve a line that is continually threatened with closure.

In medieval times Lambley must have been a comparatively flourishing village, for near the river there stood a small Benedictine nunnery founded by Adam de Tindale and his wife in the twelfth century, sacked by William Wallace in 1295 or 1296, and finally dissolved by Henry VIII.

Since the flood of 1769 nothing now remains with the exception of one of the bells, which has found its way into the minaret-like turret of the modern church.

5

North Tyne

In the old days, no part of Northumberland, and few other parts of the Border, could compare in ill-doing with North Tynedale. It was in the time of Henry VIII that Richard Fox, Bishop of Durham, was finally stung into action and, following repeated forays into his bishopric, issued a "Monition against the notorious robbers of Tynedale" in which he excommunicated great numbers of them by name. It was of no avail, and right up to the Union of the Crowns in 1603, the Charltons, Milburns, Dodds and Robsons who inhabited the valley were accustomed to raid their unfortunate neighbours, both of Scotland and England, with fine impartiality. It was not until 1771 in fact, that the Newcastle Company of Merchant Adventurers relaxed their rule forbidding its members, on pain of paying a fine of twenty pounds, from accepting apprentices from these parts.

A glance at the map should be enough to explain why the inhabitants of North Tyne were so obstreperous. Once north of Bellingham you become pretty well isolated—perhaps insulated is a better word—from the rest of England, while remaining accessible to Scotland. Moreover, apart from the haughs immediately bordering the river, the land is very poor indeed. Add to these geographical factors the very much larger population who, in medieval and Tudor times, had to make a living from the land, and it is easy to appreciate the temption to make both ends meet by rustling other people's cattle.

Isolation, poverty and a state of almost permanent warfare did little to encourage the creation of villages, attractive or otherwise, and it is hardly surprising that for most of its length the

North Tyne valley can boast little that is more than a couple of hundred years old. As one follows the river towards its source in the Border bogs of Deadwater, indeed, it becomes increasingly obvious that the replacement of the crude dwellings and bastles of the past has left one of the most historically significant parts of Northumberland with villages that are mainly utilitarian.

Strictly speaking, the first village of North Tynedale, though quite unrepresentative of the valley proper, is Wall. Travelling north along the Corn Road on its way from Hexham to Alnmouth, and approaching the Roman Wall, there is nothing much to be seen apart from a few houses and a hotel—the 'Hadrian'—that is much patronized by those who wish to dine out. Turn off the road to the east, however, and there appears before you a whin-covered hillside, terraced by sheep, below which nestles a delightful village built round a village green. At the north end are clustered particularly attractive single-storey houses and, on an island in the middle, the church, the reading-room and another house or two. Like so many villages near Hexham, Wall shows every sign of housing weekenders and commuters as well as the regulars, and very pleasant they must find it, for this is a noticeably well-kept village.

Most people would regard North Tynedale proper as starting at Chollerford bridge, where the Military Road, having descended Brunton Bank, crosses first the Corn Road and then the North Tyne itself. Here on the river bank is that delightful hotel, the 'George', and just round the corner, as it were, the village of Humshaugh, originally founded by a gentleman with the unfortunate name of Hun. Writers about Northumberland tend to hurry through Humshaugh, intent on describing Haughton Castle and the paper mill, while leaving the village to be always the bridesmaid, never the blushing bride. This is hardly fair for, after the first shock of the council houses and smart new bungalows that line a modern green, it opens out into a delightful little place, well supplied with trees, a pleasant Georgian manor house in red brick and another house with nice twisted chimneys.

In the latter years of the eighteenth century a paper mill was set up at nearby Haughton, and here it was that the paper was made for the forged banknotes which the Duke of York took with him on his ill-fated expedition to Flanders. This was generally thought at the time to be not quite cricket. How our ancestors would "stare and stretch their eyes" to see how war is conducted a century and a half later!

In 1816 the village of Haughton was demolished in order to make a park for the castle, and the inhabitants migrated to Humshaugh. And to Simonburn, some four miles away, where Sigmund had once planted his homestead beside the Stream. For long enough, as in Hexhamshire, the King's writ did not run in Tynedale, a regality separate from the rest of Northumberland, which at one time formed part of the private estates of the Scottish kings, and for which, when it suited them, they did homage. So out of hand did the reivers of Tynedale finally become that when, in the reign of Elizabeth I, the living of Simonburn was offered to the Rev. Mr Crackenthorp of Oxford, he refused point-blank to accept it, "deeming his body unable to live in so troublesome a place, and his nature not well brooking the perverse nature of so crooked a people."

Modern Simonburn is one of the most delectable villages in the county, having been rebuilt as an estate village in 1760 when the original, which stood somewhat nearer the Tyne, was demolished to build nearby Nunwick Hall. Many of the houses are of the single-storey, bothy type, built round an extensive green which is graced, among other trees, by a noble horse-chestnut. At weekends in the 'season', families come from as far afield as Tynemouth and Whitley Bay to pick the Simonburn conkers, which seem to have inherited something of the durability of those "Tynedale thieves", who used to make their Keeper's life such a misery.

Here, in the eighteenth century, John Wallis served as curate when conducting the researches that led to his *History and Description of Northumberland*. Here also, and at about the same time, lived George Pickering, the author of "Donocht Head", a poem of which Burns said he would have given ten pounds to be the author.

Others have been happy here. One day I talked to a council workman, originally a Durham miner, who had lived in Simonburn for the last seven years. Little had changed in that time, he said, except for an old barn being converted to a weekend cottage. He was quite content, as were most of the villagers, he thought, but there were minor afflictions. Once there had been a pub here, called the 'Red Lion', but the squire of the day had closed it because the workers on the estate spent too much time there, and it had been converted into two dwelling-houses. If only there was somewhere nearer than Wark (some five miles away) where he could have a game of dominoes, or place a bet, and if he were able to race his pigeons once more, he wouldn't call King Dick his uncle.

As befitted what was such an enormous parish there is a fine three-storeyed rectory, which was erected in 1666, presumably to take the place of a peel tower, in which it used to be customary for incumbents to protect themselves from the Scots and sometimes, sad to say, from their own parishioners. It is to St Mungo, the Scottish saint who is also known as St Kentigern, that the church, and incidentally the Holy Well in the Rector's Dene, are dedicated; a reminder that the church was mainly built in the thirteenth century at a time when the valley was more Scottish than English.

To the west of the North Tyne lies a great expanse of what was once, at any rate, moorland, reaching right up to the Irthing, and into Cumbria. It was over these moors that the reivers from Liddesdale rode on their unlawful occasions and, in more peaceful times, the Scottish drovers herded their great armies of cattle towards the fair at Stagshaw Bank or on their way to the pastures of East Anglia.

The advent of railways put an end to the droving industry and now the wastes are covered, like so much of the North Tyne valley, by trees—in this case Wark Forest. In a clearing stands what looks on the map like just another isolated farm, but is actually the village of Stonehaugh. The way to it lies along an unexpectedly good road, straightened and resurfaced to take the forestry traffic, that wanders over some five miles of moorland and then drops down through the trees to the wide Haugh by the Warks Burn that gives the place its name. Here by the water's edge the Forestry Commission has thoughtfully provided rustic seats, totem poles and all the amenities of a splendid playground where children can disport themselves. It is, in fact, a designated Picnic Area, and signposted as such.

The village itself has been built comparatively recently to house forestry workers and their families, and it has not yet had time to settle into its surroundings. Well-mown grass graces the rows of buff-coloured houses and does a great deal to improve the look of the place, while a wind-vane in the shape of a fox swings jauntily in the breeze alongside a football pitch. A repair shop for the forestry machinery, a village hall and a shop-cum-post office complete the picture so far as the villagers are concerned. There is another side to the place, however, in the shape of a caravan site, and a number of chalets where anyone who wants to get away from it all can spend their holidays. People from as far afield as Japan have turned up here, bringing to this isolated spot much-needed contacts with the world outside.

Forestry workers tend to a considerable extent to come and go, for the job attracts townies looking for fresh air and the certainty of a house, not realizing that they may have to sacrifice some of the bright lights to which they and their families have been accustomed. The nearest pub and church are at Wark, five miles away, so that the possession of a car is almost a necessity, while a bus calls for the schoolchildren. Yet the 'regulars' seem very contented with their lot for, to the countryman, there are a number of compensations. "Did you ever see so many beautiful shades of green?" asked the lady who keeps the post office, pointing over the open countryside to the north. And behind all the greens lay the blue haze of the Otterburn moors and the hills of Liddesdale. To someone like herself who had spent seven years at Stonehaugh after half a lifetime in the urban desolation of Blyth, it was all (or nearly all) sheer bliss.

For a place with the history, and at one time the importance, of Wark (sometimes distinguished from the place of that name on the banks of the Tweed as Wark-on-Tyne) the village is sadly disappointing, for little remains to remind one of the past. It was here for instance that Alfwald, that "just and pious king" succumbed to what, for the kings of Northumbria, seems to have been an occupational hazard, and was duly murdered. Later the Normans built a castle near the river, on what is still known—though it is partly levelled now—as the Mote Hill. Tradition has it that most, if not all, of the hill was artificially created, even the women and children being pressed into service to carry 'lapfuls' of soil. That this was actually the case is more or less proved by the fact that, although in Alfwald's day the place was known as

E

Scyteceastre, its name was subsequently changed to denote a Work, or Earthwork. In Northumberland we tend to rhyme 'work' with 'bark' and this is how we still pronounce Wark-on-Tyne, though if you want to speak the Queen's English, you may of course, prefer to rhyme it with 'pork'.

When Wark was the capital of the barony of Tynedale, the centre for a population anything up to five times what it is today, and therefore a much larger and more important place, it stretched as far north as the Houxty Burn. Here, not far from where Abel Chapman, the great naturalist, used to live, the name of the Kirk Field commemorates the spot where the church of St Michael of Wark used to stand; while to the south of the village such names as Park End and Latterford Gates mark the limits of its Great Park. Later on, the barony formed part of the enormous estates of the Radcliffes, later Earls of Derwentwater, and passed with the rest to Greenwich Hospital after the Fifteen. One of these days someone will write an account of the activities of its Commissioners in Northumberland, for their influence on the county has been vast. Farmsteads, smelt mills, roads, vicarages and churches were built by them, including St Matthew's at Wark.

Nowadays the village yields pride of place to Bellingham (pronounced of course Bellinjum)—the Village of the Dwellers on the Hill. In view of the latter's importance, both administrative and cultural, it is tempting to call it a town and pass on. Nevertheless, despite the number of schools, of places of worship, and of pubs, the size of its population together with its rustic atmosphere clearly establish it as a village. In point of fact it is only the vastness of the area it serves that might lead one to think otherwise, with people for instance, as far afield as Byrness eighteen miles away in Redesdale, and Kielder, another twenty miles up North Tyne, depending on Bellingham for a doctor.

On entering the place from Wark, the first landmark one encounters is Brown Rigg, one of the few boarding schools run by the Education Authority; but it is the fire station that really catches the eye, closely followed by the Catholic church, after which the village soon opens out into an impressive square (except that it isn't square), lined with pubs, of which the 'Rose and Crown' is the biggest and the 'Black Bull' the oldest. Then comes another fine modern school and the road that crosses the moor known as Hareshaw Common, on its way to Otterburn. This is sheep country and it is at Bellingham that what was once a great wool fair has given way to an agricultural show which continues to exercise a powerful fascination for those like the old man in the song.

Aa's an auld shepherd, an' Aa live oot-bye,
An Aa seldom see owt but the sheep and the kye,
So Aa ses to wor Betsy 'Aa think Aa will go
And hev a bit look at the Bellingham Show'.

But year in, year out, it is St Cuthbert's church that provides the chief interest of the place. In the days of the Border reivers the old church was continually set on fire, and it is not surprising, therefore, that at the beginning of the seventeenth century, only a few years after "the thieves of Liddesdale spoiled the townsmen and brake the cross", it was rebuilt with a roof of heavy stone slabs supported by no less than twenty arches, also of stone, which (hopefully) left nothing for the Scots to ignite. Outside, in the churchyard are buried Dodds, Milburns, Robsons and even some of the Armstrongs and Elliots who were as often as not their deadly enemies. It was in 1711 that William Charlton of the Bower—and therefore known to all and sundry as Bowrie Charlton—killed Henry Widdrington of Buteland in a quarrel. This was in the days when the law demanded that Catholics, such as the Charltons, attended the parish church at least once a quarter. In order to get some of their own back, the Widdringtons had the dead man buried in front of the Charltons' pew as a gentle reminder to Bowrie whenever he was forced to come to church.

On the north side lies a long stone shaped like a pedlar's pack, with lines to represent the cords. Some time in the eighteenth century Colonel Ridley, who had made his fortune in India, was living in one of the Charlton houses, Lee Hall near Wark. One winter's night when the family was in London, a pedlar begged a night's lodging and when the servant refused, asked if he might leave his pack in the house. This, Alice, the servant, allowed him to do. When she saw the pack begin to move, however, she hastily shouted for one of the farm hands who, seizing a gun used for scaring rooks, promptly let fly. When blood began to ooze from the pack the two of them realized that their worst suspicions had been confirmed, namely that a thief had been planted in the house; and they sent for help. Some twenty-five of the neighbours answered the call and, as soon as they professed themselves ready, Edward, the hind, sounded the silver horn (some say it was a whistle) that he had found on the body.

Thereupon the rest of the gang duly appeared, only to be greeted by a volley which left a number of them lying on the ground. By the next day the bodies had disappeared, but it soon became evident that there were many respectable families in the neighbourhood that were short of some of their members. It is the body that was found in the pack that is reputed to be buried here.

From Bellingham you have two choices if you wish to continue up the North Tyne and, if you are wise, you will follow the road along the east bank of the river below Hareshaw Common as far, and only as far, as Lanehead and its neighbour, Greenhaugh. Like many other parts of Northumberland this is a land of moor and fell, of stone walls, Blackface sheep and hardy Galloway cattle. Now that the population of the valley has shrunk drastically compared to the days when overpopulation begat so much robbery and violence, there are no villages of any size to be found; just tiny hamlets boasting a church, a pub or a school (but seldom all together) and serving a population scattered for miles around. Nor is any of them particularly ancient—the Scots have seen to that.

Greenhaugh is typical of these: just a few plain stone houses straggling along the road, too far 'outbye' for commuters; insufficiently attractive to weekenders. Really the place should be considered in conjunction with Tarset, just a mile or so below, for the latter provides sustenance for the soul in the shape of a chapel, while Greenhaugh provides it for the mind and stomach, in the shape of a tiny school and a pub—the Hollybush Inn. The crossroads known as Lanehead mark the place where the old drove road that ran down from Scotland across the Coquet Valley, through Bardon Mill and Blanchland, crossed that which came down the North Tyne by way of Bellingham and Corbridge. Nobody seems sure whether Tarset was where a man named Tir had his 'sete' or Fold, or whether the Fold was named after the Resinous Wood of which it was constructed. Near the crossroads a green mound is all that remains of the castle of the Red Comyn of Badenoch, whom Robert Bruce killed in 1306.

From Lanehead the motorist who has been forewarned crosses the river by a bridge that, like others in the valley, shows signs of being strengthened in readiness to bear the traffic to the projected Kielder Reservoir that is designed to supply with water the factories, not of Tyneside but, believe it or not, of Teeside, some eighty miles away.

The alternative is to continue up the east bank but, unless one has a passenger and an active one at that, this is pure purgatory, for a succession of eight gates means no less than sixteen descents by the unlucky driver in order to open and shut them. And when you get to Falstone, what do you find? Not the Multicoloured Stone that the name suggests, but a huddle of rather undistinguished-loking houses, church, pub and, of all things a railway station, now of course defunct. It was here that on 10th December 1864, not long after the Border Counties railway was opened, a goods train left the rails killing both driver and fireman. But how delightful it must once have been to puff up and down the North Tyne Valley on this line that later became part of the North British network. Alas, with such a small population and only the coalmine at Plashetts to provide any serious freight, it could never have paid.

From Stannersburn, where stands the drovers' pub known as the 'Blackcock', one drives through "the largest man-made forest in Europe", taking good care to avoid the deer that gambol about the road, until you reach the forestry village which takes its name from the Violent Water of the Kielder Burn. Apart from the noble viaduct (now, thank goodness, to be preserved in perpetuity) and the Duke's shoting lodge known as Kielder Castle, the only edifice of note in what is otherwise much like any other forestry village is the fine community centre.

Crossing the river at Wark brings you to what must surely be one of the highest concentrations of British camps in the country, with names such as Carry House, Goodwife Hot, Garret Hot, Countess Park, Mill Knock, Buteland and Nightfolds. Right in the middle of them, on an eminence four hundred feet above the east bank of the river, lies the Bright Clearing now known as the village of Birtley, a cheerful little place with attractive old houses grouped round a large village green. St Giles' church is reputedly Norman, but very much restored. Built into the chancel wall is a stone worth seeing. On it are inscribed an Iona cross of the seventh century—that is to say one with crossbars on the end of the arms—and the letters O R P E in the form of a square, which, if read the right way, might represent *"Orate pro* R . . . E . . .". Almost opposite stands what was once the vicarage, now greatly modernized and improved. In the garden, with a view over the river and far to the west, stand the remains of what has been known at different times as Birtley Hall and Birtley Castle. They measure, so far as one can make out, about fifty feet each way and bear on one wall the initials J.H. (probably one of the Herons who lived at Chipchase Castle not far away) and the date 1611. It is all rather mysterious, for if this is the original date, it can hardly be a peel tower, for the Union of the Crowns had by then materially reduced the risk of being attacked by Scottish (or English) reivers; nor do the rounded corners fit the bill. Yet the canon balls dug up in the garden point to the place having undergone some kind of siege—perhaps in the Civil War.

If you follow the east side of the valley, the next village is Gunnerton. Here a certain Gunwara once made his home, since when the place has been chiefly famous for its quarries, carved out of the Great Whin Sill that runs right across Northumberland.

Like Birtley, the place is surrounded with British camps, including one a couple of miles to the north now known as Pity Me —a corruption of the British *beddan maes*, meaning the Field of the Graves. The village itself, a mixture of stone houses and brick villas, is not particularly interesting except perhaps for the extraordinary church. This was designed by a gentleman named Hall, who (perhaps luckily for the architectural profession) later took Holy Orders, then joined the Catholic Church and finished his days as a hermit.

It looks as if the inhabitants of Gunnerton and Barrasford have never been very clear in their minds what belonged to which, for Barrasford Quarries are nearer to Gunnerton than to their parent and so, until it was closed down, was Barrasford Sanatorium. Part of Barrasford lies along the bank of the river; part of it, including a number of council houses and old people's homes, on the road that leads upwards to the station. A little further to the west runs the Fell Lane, once known as the Chishill Way, though whether because gravel was taken up it from the river, or because the original track was itself gravelly, it is now difficult to say. About half the council houses are occupied by families who derive a living from the local quarries, but a number of the older houses, clustered round what is more a field than a green, have been improved over the years, and now house retired business people. Indeed the increasing proportion of old to young is causing a good deal of concern here, as in many other villages.

It is the Ford by the Grove that gives Barrasford its name, and for long enough there has been a primitive ferry here that has enabled many of the quarrymen living in Humshaugh to leave their bicycles near Haughton Castle and cross the river to work. With a steadily decreasing number of customers it has become uneconomic to employ a ferryman. A small boat remains, though there is no guarantee that it will be manned; and the overhead rope and the safety wire from which a line was fastened to it have disappeared.

Don't on any account miss Chollerton, the Homestead by Ceola's Ford (Chollerford) for, though small, there is much to see, including a big farmstead with a pleasant house and the remains of a windmill in the farmyard. In the centre of the village, where the Corn Road leaves the line of the river, on its way to the sea, there is an open space that was once a station yard when Chollerton was the first stop out of Hexham on the Border Counties railway. Here the station-master's house, and that adjoining, remain much as they were. The station itself, however, has been turned into a most attractive residence, which quite enhances the look of the place. Opposite it stands a church with a curious wooden spire. A lot of it is eighteenth-century; but the south arcade is composed of Roman pillars, in contrast to the fourteenth-century piers on the north; the rearmost of them, incorporated in the West Wall, being noticeably out of the vertical. In addition to the thirteenth-century font there is another which was originally a Roman altar.

By the lychgate stands something you will not find in any of the guide books; notably a low building with two doors, an old stone-slab roof and a 'loupin-on styen'* in front. Originally it was a stable for parishioners' horses, and shelter for corpses brought from a distance. For a time it even served as a post office. In the churchyard stands a tombstone, the inscription on which reads:

In memory of John Saint of Cocklaw Fulling
Mill, who died June 5, 1837.

Nothing extraordinary in that, you might think, but the stone also bears a representation of the fulling mill itself, accurate in every detail, and showing besom, spade and other tools of the fuller's trade leaning against the front of the building. Now, fullers—that is to say the people who cleansed and filled out the cloth once it was woven—always used to be known as walkers, and it is therefore no surprise to find the old mill (which looks more like a couple of cottages, standing by the roadside to the east of the railway viaduct) alluded to as the Walk Mill.

* Mounting stone.

6

Redesdale

W H E N Agricola set out to conquer the North of England, his first
thought was to build a strategic road from Eboracum—in other
words York—up to the Forth and beyond. Running through Cat-
terick and Piercebridge, it entered Northumberland at Ebchester;
then on through Whittonstall to Riding Mill. Thence for some
thirty miles, until it reaches Rochester, it followed almost exactly
what is now the line of the A68 road which runs through Corbridge, Jedburgh and Lauder to Edinburgh. For years the Roman
road was known, by association, as Watling Street, but it has now
resumed its much older name of Dere Street, the paved road or
street that ran up through Deira (the more southerly of the
Anglian kingdoms) into Bernicia, or what we now know as Northumberland plus the countryside up to the Forth.

In Northumberland nearly all hills are either 'banks' or, in
placenames, 'laws', so it is up Stagshaw Bank you must climb
from Corbridge if you want to follow Dere Street northwards. At
the top you will find a pub, a garage and an innocent-looking
roundabout. That is all. Yet this was once one of the key points of
Northumberland, for it was here at Portgate that Hadrian's men
left a port, or gap, in the wall through which Dere Street might
pass—in effect the main sallyport for expeditions against Scotland. But it is more than that, for it is here that it also crosses
the Military Road which follows the line of the Wall, while on the
fell nearby there was held for hundreds of years—in fact up to the
early days of the twentieth century—a fair for horses and cattle
that was one of the biggest in England. And it was here, along the
crumbling Dere Street, that the Scottish drovers brought their

cattle from the trysts of Crieff and Falkirk in the course of their long trek south.

A little way northwards, near the Five Lane Ends where Dere Street is crossed by the Corn Road, lies Colwell. It was one of the idiosyncrasies of our Anglian ancestors that they were wont to call places the Cold Well (though any other kind of spring must have been rare indeed) and this is one of them; now a village that is little more than a cluster of farms.

Back to Dere Street, which proceeds unconcernedly on its way, straight as a dart, up one bank and down another, so that it is not corners that the prudent motorist must look for, but an apparently endless succession of blind crests. From the Five Lane Ends it is some ten miles to the next village of any consequence, West Woodburn, past Colt Crag reservoir; past the little farm of Waterfalls, where the burn dives underground, and where Tom Forster and the Earl of Derwentwater first raised the Jacobite flag in 1715; and past a number of small quarries from which Agricola took his stone for the road. Past the Roman signal station and their camp at Fourlaws, and past a rather dreary line of houses and what looks like the remains of an ancient peel tower. I don't imagine that one motorist in a thousand ever stops here unless he has to. Yet this has a history too, though it does not go back more than a century, for here is Ridsdale, where iron ore was once mined, where the future Lord Armstrong set up an ironworks, and where he tested the guns that made his name. A plain looking pub, appropriately called 'The Gun', together with the ruins of the iron-works (which are not a peel tower after all), the twenty or so houses and a tiny general store-cum-post-office are all that remain to remind one of such an important episode in the history of warfare. Except that the tradition of testing military equipment still survives, for it is here that Vickers (Armstrong's successor) still try out their tanks. When the works came to an end it became painfully obvious that in such a barren countryside it was unlikely that fresh occupants would be found, so the tenants were offered their houses at the price of one year's rent—£14! Few, if any, accepted, but since then the houses have been bought very cheaply by people working in nearby quarries and at the sawmill a little to the south. Furthermore, their very cheapness, together with the chance of obtaining generous grants to bring them up to date, have tempted weekenders to invest in what a few years ago would have seemed a most unlikely spot. So Ridsdale has risen again like a phoenix from the ashes of its furnaces.

> And near the spot that gave me name,
> The moated mound of Risingham,
> Where Reed upon her margin sees
> Sweet Woodburne's cottages and trees,
> Some ancient sculptor's art has shown
> An outlaw's image on the stone.

So much for Bertram Risingham in Scott's "Rokeby", who was referring to the first settlement at Woodburn of which we have any knowledge—the Roman fort of Habitancum, the remains of which cover some four-and-a-half acres just to the west of the present A68 as it approaches the River Rede. Here also are to be seen the remains of the causeway that carried the Roman road over the marshy ground near by. A Roman milestone that once served as a gatepost for the 'Bay Horse' has since been re-discovered and erected once more in the grounds of the inn. Later there arrived the Risingas, or followers of Risa, who created a Village (no doubt of the Roman stone) and gave it their name, Risingham; a place that now survives only as an adjunct to West Woodburn.

"Sweet Woodburne's" cottages now lie roughly in the form of a cross, most of them along the A68, which here descends some 350 feet to the bridge and then rises again. There are others, however, scattered along the river bank, and here, on the road to East Woodburn stand the trees in question, with the Rede, at its loveliest here, rippling and flashing between them on its way to join the North Tyne. The figure cut in the rock to which Scott referred was the famous Robin of Risingham, a rough sketch of what appeared to be a Roman centurion, but is now, alas, no more.

From West Woodburn the road pursues its way steadily northwards across Corsenside Common where, about a mile from the village, it is traversed by the old drove road to Tarset, which crosses the Rede by a delightful old bridge of two arches which is well worth pausing to admire. The only difficulty is the number of gates that have to be opened (and closed) on the way. Then on again as far as the farm of Elishaw, where the A68 is joined by the road from Newcastle through Otterburn.

At Rochester, however, the turnpike at last separates from Dere Street and runs on over the Carter Bar into Scotland, while the Roman road continues almost due north to cross the Cheviots in the form of a track known as Gamelspath. By no stretch of imagination can Rochester be called a village, but together with High Rochester and Horsley, a mile further back, it is undoubtedly a centre for the surrounding farms and the best we can do in such a bare countryside; for this is white fell, that is to say moorland that is covered with whitish bent, as opposed to black fell which bears heather and ling. In fact it is an area of big sheep farms, one of which, the Experimental Husbandry Farm of the Ministry of Agriculture, includes within its bounds the pitiful remains of Evistones, once a village that boasted five or six bastle (fortified) houses and no doubt a number of cottages as well. On the other side of the road is Redesdale Camp which, with the camp near Otterburn, houses the soldiery using the artillery ranges that stretch eastwards to the Coquet.

Of the three it is Horsley that provides both church and pub. The former is small and comparatively modern, though with a Roman altar—presumably taken from the marching camp nearby —in the porch. The latter (the 'Redesdale Arms') reminds one of the story of Parcy Reed of Troughend near Otterburn, who incurred the enmity of the Halls of Girsonfield by his appointment at the end of the sixteenth century as Keeper of Redesdale. Accordingly the Halls betrayed him to his deadly enemies, the Scottish Croziers, with the result that his remains had to be taken home in a sheet. For years after the event any of the Halls who asked for hospitality within their own county might expect to find the cheese placed before them upside down—an accepted sign of disrespect. It was well into the nineteenth century, indeed, when a traveller asked the landlord of this very inn at Horsley what was his name. "Wey, noo," answered the innkeeper, "Aa winna disguise me neame: me neame's Ha' . . . Tommy Ha'," and wept copiously into his beer, denying all the while any relationship with the Halls of Girsonfield.

Rochester itself consists of a sprinkling of houses along, and to the east of, the main road; the chief interest being centred in the old school lately converted to a smart dwelling-house, complete with sun-parlour. The porch, which remains undisturbed, is constructed of Roman stones, including a couple of the large stone balls used as ammunition for the *ballistae*, or giant catapults, from the fort of Bremenium (High Rochester) a quarter of a mile away. Once one of the finest of all the Roman forts, and one that has given the village its name of the Camp frequented by Rooks, there is little now to be seen. Its centre, however, still serves as a kind of village green, round which are ranged a number of cottages, the remains of a peel tower built (naturally) of Roman stone, and the original guard chamber standing nearly ten feet high.

Just before leaving the Redesdale forest a Ness, or Nose of land, sticks out towards the Rede, on which there must once have stood a Borran, or burial place, but which now carries the Pennine Way as it meanders across the Cheviots. It is from this hill that the original hamlet of Byrness, and the present forestry village, took their name. The latter is built in much the same style as others erected by the Forestry Commission, but the original specification was never fully carried out. There is a good-looking primary school (if that is still the right title), a Co-operative store, a village hall and post office. There are also—Byrness being in the Northumberland National Park, as well as a convenient stopping place on the Pennine Way—an information centre and a youth hostel.

A little way down the main road ("back over", as we would say) stands a garage, the last pub in England and a most attractive little church. Only 29 by 18 feet, and roofed with the old stone slabs, you could hardly wish for anything more delightful. Surely a local mason must have been told to build out of his head a church reflecting all that is most typical of its surroundings. There it crouches, tiny, solid, stark and dependable among its sheltering trees, almost as if it had grown out of the soil itself.

A thousand navvies took fifteen years to construct the Catcleugh reservoir a little further up the valley, and during that time there were sixty-four deaths among the workers and their families, though few of them from any but natural causes. Commemorating the dead is a window in the church showing the men working on the reservoir, an engine and trucks alongside them, and a boy

waiting for his father with his 'bait' wrapped up in a handker-
chief.

From Byrness there is only one way to go, and that is back again,
this time eschewing the right fork at Elishaw and continuing towards Otterburn. Almost a mile before you get to the village
proper, there appears for some inexplicable reason the village
school. Then, on the same side of the road the so-called Percy
Cross. This is an upright, pointed pillar standing on its original
round base, though the cross itself appears to have been broken
off at some date.

It was in 1388 that a Scottish army of 5–6,000 men under the
Earls of Douglas, March and Moray, on the way back from harrying the Bishopric of Durham, called in at Newcastle, but the
defences proved too strong for them. That hero of Northumbrian history, Henry Percy—more commonly known as Harry
Hotspur—challenged Douglas to single combat and, losing his
spear in the encounter, set off in pursuit. After a forced march, he
caught up with the Scots, who had paused to besiege (though
without success) the tower of Otterburn. The resulting battle,
fought by moonlight, ended in the death of Douglas but the
defeat of the English, who had been committed without any chance
to rest. It was to mark the spot where Douglas fell that the cross
was originally erected, but was moved from its old position (a
little further north) in 1777.

The present Otterburn Tower bears little resemblance to the
place that Douglas failed to capture, though it incorporates many
of the old stones. It was originally built by the Umfravilles, who
had been granted the lordship of Redesdale by the Conqueror on
condition that they protected its inhabitants from marauders *and
wolves*. Later it passed to that noted Redesdale family, the Halls,
who were connected, of course, with the "fause Haa's of Girson-
fields" nearby. One of them, John Hall, better known for his
exploits, despite his position as a magistrate, as Mad Jack Hall,
was captured with the Earl of Derwentwater in the Fifteen. It was
all a mistake, he protested. He had been riding home one day
from a magistrates' meeting in Coquetdale, when he suddenly
found himself surrounded by the rebels, who insisted on him and
his servant accompanying them, though he himself was unarmed
and had only seven-and-six in his pocket. The Judge, however,

would have none of this, and Mad Jack was duly executed at Tyburn, where he and Parson Paul "died in a rage, denying everything they had owned in their petitions."

Here also for many years lived that delightful historian of the county, Howard Pease. But it was Robert Roxby, from the Newcastle bank in which he slaved who, above all men, has sung the praises of Redesdale, carolling in "The Lay of the Redewater Minstrel" of

> Thy ferny braes, thy streamlets sweet
> ... enchanting Otterburn.

Largely rebuilt in the nineteenth century, the village can no longer be regarded as enchanting, but its amenities include a new building estate and a fine Working Men's Club at its east end. It is the Percy Arms, however, that really makes the place. Long, low and whitewashed, with a pleasant garden to the south, it is generally full of fishing and shooting parties.

Chief (apart from the Rede itself) among the "streamlets sweet" of which Robert Roxby sang is the tiny Otter Burn that gives the place its name and which, before it joins the river, passes the famous woollen mill that, starting out as a fulling mill, has for long enough exported Otterburn tweeds, scarves and rugs to all parts of the world. To this place comes the blackface wool of the neighbouring moors—the Ottercops, Billsmoor and the rest—to be woven by a family that has worked the mill for generations. It is not so long since an old lady at Cambo was able to recall being sent out as a child to collect wool from the hedges. "Then it was sent to Otterburn mills and carded, and then my mother spun it on her big wheel . . . if it was for blankets, it went back to Otterburn to be woven."

Whereas the fame of Otterburn is largely derived from the battle that was fought there, and which, incidentally, was quite a different affair to Chevy Chase, with which the ballad makers have confused it, it is Elsdon, some four miles to the east that has always been regarded as the capital of Redesdale.

It was in 1702 that the Rev. Charles Dodgson appeared there to begin a three-year spell as rector before becoming Bishop of Ossory. "Modern Elsdon . . ." he wrote to the Duke, "is a very small village consisting of a tower which the inhabitants call a castle, an inn for the refreshment of Scotch carriers, five little farm houses, and a few wretched cottages, about ten in all."

A few of the better houses remain much the same as they did in Dodgson's time, though the tower (of which more anon) has been somewhat altered. The little 'Crown Inn' was rebuilt in 1729.

One's first impression of the place is of pleasant-looking dwellings plonked down higgledy-piggledy in a kind of rough triangle, leaving in the middle a village green some acres in extent and criss-crossed with roads that enter from five different directions. In the summer, with its white railings and profusion of streams, it is a delightful place. When the snows come it is rather a different matter. As George Chatt, the Hexham poet put it,

> Hae ye ivver been at Elsdon?
> The world's unfinished neuk;
> It stands amang the hungry hills
> An' wears a frozen leuk.
> The Elsdon folk, like diein' stags,
> At every stranger stare,
> An' heather broth an' curlew eggs
> Ye'll get for supper there.

Certainly Elsdon stands among the hungry hills, but is itself named after the Valley once inhabited by a gentleman named Elli who, for no particular reason, is reputed to have been a Danish giant who terrorised the countryside for miles around. The poet, however, was not the only person to mention the cold. Wrote Dodgson, "I lay in the parlour between two beds* to keep me from being frozen to death, for as we keep open house the winds enter from every quarter and are apt to creep into bed with one".

It is hardly to be wondered at that he felt the cold, for his vicarage was the fourteenth-century Vicar's Peel, a building almost, if not quite, exclusive to Northumberland. In the days of the Scottish wars, and of marauding bands of reivers, it would be the natural place for the parson to live, but times change and the vicarage is now a private house. One of its occupants, at least, had to endure worse things than the cold. It was Percival Reed of Troughend (perhaps the son of the murdered Parcy) who became so annoyed with the parson of Elsdon that, calling him "base priest

* Feather mattresses.

and stinking castrel", he pulled the reverend gentleman's beard. For this lapse he was bidden to appear in Elsdon church and publicly acknowledge the error of his ways. Pretending illness, he got his unfortunate wife to stand in for him.

On an island in the green stands St Cuthbert's church with its queer bell-cote and stumpy spire, part of it early thirteenth, but mainly of the fourteenth century. Worth looking at is the Roman tombstone from High Rochester which rests against a pillar in the north aisle, and which states that "Julia Lucilla had this stone erected to her very meritorious husband, an inspector under the surveyor of the Flaminian Way". When the church was repaired in the last century, three horses' skulls were found in the masonry above the bells. What their purpose was is anybody's guess. Was it to improve the tone of the bells, to act as a charm against lightning, or what?

A find more easily explained came to light in 1810, when a whole lot of earth was removed from outside the north wall of the church, revealing over a hundred skeletons buried in a double row. All the evidence (and it is considerable) points to their being the bones of men who died in the battle of Otterburn.

Finally, for there is much to see at Elsdon, at the north end of the village there lie the enormous mounds, partly or wholly man-made, known as the Mote Hills; the remains of what was once perhaps the finest motte-and-bailey castle in Northumberland, built by the Norman lords of Redesdale and inhabited by such famous Umfravilles as Robert-with-the-beard and Robin-mend-the-market.

F

7

The Heartland

S o far we have looked at villages either in the more 'civilized' (or at any rate tamer) parts of Northumberland, or else in areas that are particularly wild, and nothing very much in between. However, between the Simonsides to the north, the Ottercops to the west and the Roman Wall to the south there lies a countryside that is noticeably different from either. In geological terms it has been described as "a region of gentle scarps, formed by the outcrops of the chief sandstones and limestones, with deep slopes towards the south-east". Compared to the coastal plain to the east of it, or to the Tyne Valley, the land is not particularly suitable for arable crops, though from the time of the Napoleonic wars onward, it has often been pressed into service to grow corn, with varying amounts of success. With a fairly high rainfall, stiffish soil and elevations varying between three and eight hundred feet above sea level, this is in fact a district that is more fitted for stock farming and it includes some of the most suitable pastures in Northumberland for the finishing of cattle (many of them imported from Ireland) and the production of fat lambs.

The rolling Cheviot hills, the wet and craggy Pennines, the pit country of the south east, the moors and the Tyne valley—all can be duplicated elsewhere in England. But this—the Heartland of Northumberland—is unique. That is not to say that it is particularly beautiful or particularly fertile or particularly anything. It is just Northumberland, windswept and bleak, except in the little valleys where there are to be found some magnificent trees. Unspoilt by industry or tourism, it is a quiet land of open spaces, grey farmsteads and small, scattered villages, many of them the creation of the large estates.

Having said all that, what are we to make of Ponteland where, for all practical purposes the Heartland begins, but which conforms to none of these criteria? It was the railway from Newcastle, opened in 1905 and only recently closed (so far as Ponteland is concerned), that inspired a complete modernization of what in those days was a rustic village of considerable character but, apart from the church, the 'Blackbird Inn', the Old Vicarage and the remains of a peel tower, of no particular beauty. Since then the nature of the place has been transformed by the birth of a stepsister in the shape of Darras Hall. This was the name of a nearby farm once owned by, and named after, the Norman family of D'Arreyns, but bought by a land development company formed to create a kind of garden city which would provide a slap-up dormitory for Newcastle. Very wisely the directors stipulated that the land should be built over gradually and that the size of the plots sold should be large enough to preserve a semblance of privacy.

Through Ponteland itself runs the little river Pont on its way to join the Blyth. Before the lakes of Prestwick Carr were drained in the last century, the river flooded to such an extent as to leave the village an Island on the Pont—hence the name. Due to its position on the road that used to run through Elsdon into Scotland, the place has had its fair share of excitement. Here, for instance, there took place a confrontation between the armies of Henry III and Alexander II which, due to the intervention of the Archbishop of York, finally resulted not in a battle but a peace treaty. Here, also, Sir Aymer de Atholl strove unsuccessfully against the Earl of Douglas on his way to the battle of Otterburn.

Since then enormous changes have taken place in Ponteland, not least during the last twenty years. A station has been and gone, though the cattle market survives. The old brewery, and the farmstead that used to occupy the middle of the village, have disappeared, the Coates Endowed School has been converted into offices, the Workhouse into a hospital and the Cottage Homes into the Northumberland College of Education. In all this, however, the village has gained far more than it has lost, and now rejoices in three banks, two large garages, a library, a clinic, a fine shopping precinct, new schools, old people's homes, and even a sports centre.

It was Mark Errington of Woolsington who built, out of the remains of the fourteenth-century bastle, a manor house, part of which is included in the 'Blackbird Inn' that still retains the seventeenth-century mullioned windows, the fireplace, and the tunnel vaulting of the original, while serving excellent food in the modern manner. Another relic of medieval times is to be found in the pathetic remains of a vicar's peel. There cannot be many villages enjoying the equivalent of four different rectories, but Ponteland does, for near the 'Blackbird' stands that rarity in Northumberland, an eighteenth-century brick house, which is in fact the Old Rectory. The stone-built edifice in whose garden the peel stands, and which now houses Council offices, used to be known as the New Rectory, while opposite the church stands a newer one still. A church, incidentally, that has attained a fresh importance from the very much increased population (including, of course, Darras Hall). One of the finest in the county, St Mary's is basically Norman, with thirteenth- and fourteenth-century additions.

Further up the Pont stands Dissington Hall, built about 1770 on the site previously occupied by an earlier house where Admiral Sir Ralph Delaval was born, who served in the battles of Beachy Head and La Hogue, and finished up in Westminster Abbey. The estate subsequently passed to the Collingwoods, a family that also provided a famous Admiral in the shape of Cuthbert, Lord Collingwood, Nelson's great friend and successor as Commander-in-Chief, Mediterranean. The village of Dalton, which takes its name from the Dale of the Pont, is nothing more than a hamlet of perhaps twenty houses approached (from the east) along the high wall, backed by rhododendrons, that shields Dissington from the public gaze. However, it does have a small church, and used once to boast a school, now converted into a dwelling house.

Originally, many of the houses (built entirely on one side of the road) were no doubt occupied by families connected with the estate. Nowadays, with their neat gardens and well-kept hedges, they are largely occupied by outsiders.

Stamfordham, on its plateau sloping down to the fledgling Pont and the marshy land to the west, is quite another kettle of fish. As one turns the corner into the village from Dalton, one's first impression is of bustling modernity. On one side stands a biggish garage; on the other a building estate that has lately supplanted—and not before time either—a number of hideous buildings in which, during the Second World War, land-girls were housed.

Another turn, however, and the full beauty of the village becomes apparent. The place is built round an extensive village green on which fairs used to be held. The original settlement appears to have been at the Heugh, now represented by little more than a single farm, about a mile to the north, and most of the present village owes its origin to the enclosure award of 1735 which settled the claims of Sir John Swinburne of Capheaton, who owned half the land, and Balliol College, Oxford, to whom most of the rest belonged. This provided, among other things, that the green of Stamfordham should be enjoyed by the landowners concerned, with "their tenants and farmers, and by the inhabitants of such houses as are or shall be built upon the said town green, with the consent and direction of Sir John Swinburne and Balliol College."

A reminder of the cattle fairs instituted in 1732 is to be found in the market cross that isn't a cross at all, but a little shelter of four arches with a stone-slabbed roof, presented to the village by Sir John Swinburne. Another is the tiny 'kitty', or lock-up, where the obstreperous were incarcerated before the modern police station was built. Here in the early days of the present century 'Nanny Blackjack' used to be restrained every fair day when she had drunk herself into oblivion. Opposite the market cross, and towering above the other houses on the north side of the village, is a three-storey stone house with a brick front, known as Cross House. It was here that our old friend James, Earl of Derwentwater, used to come to play bowls. In view of the rarity of brick buildings in Northumberland it may well be that the brick front was an inexpensive way of making the house look more exclusive than its fellows.

On the south side of the green stands the Bay Horse pub, with an outside stone stairway leading to the loft which, for so many years, served the purpose of a village hall; and the charming old house that was for long enough the abode of the village schoolmaster, but before that was itself used as a school.

Interesting though the village is in general, it is the church and vicarage that are its chief delights. St Mary's is a big church dating back to the thirteenth century, but extensively restored. To the uninitiated the solid, dumpy tower, rising only a few feet above the rest of the church, gives the impression that it is older still. Inside hangs a big banner bearing three black birds, which once hung in Henry VII's chapel in Westminster Abbey over the stall of Lord Stamfordham, made Knight Grand Cross of the Order of the Bath for his services as private secretary to Queen Victoria. He was the son of John Bigge, for many years vicar here, and himself belonging to an old Northumbrian family.

As you walk down the footpath to the Stony Ford from which the village takes its name, you pass the enormous vicarage, part of it with the typical Tudor chimneys so unusual in Northumberland. Other parts of it are eighteenth century, with finishing touches by John Dobson. Now divided into two, it has a delightful view of the tiny river, its tributary burn and the 'suburb' of Hawkwell.

From Stamfordham to Matfen is a matter of four or five miles, past a stretch of marshy land through which the infant Pont meanders, and from which one of the best-known families in Northumberland originated, taking their name from the Farm in the Fen. It was the Fenwicks, indeed, who, however unwittingly, caused the death of William III. A staunch Jacobite, Sir John Fenwick was arrested for his part in a plot against the usurper. He was duly executed and his property sequestered to the crown— including, of course, his horses. It was when mounted on one of these that William met his death after the beast, itself no doubt having Jacobite leanings, stumbled on a mole-hill and threw its rider. Hence the Jacobite toast to the "little gentleman in black velvet".

At the far end of this Fen lived a certain Matta, who gave his name to Matfen, a village whose principle adornment is the Hall, now the Northumberland Cheshire Home, where a devoted staff look after the disabled. For long enough, however, it was the home of the Blacketts, one of whom, incidentally, married Admiral Collingwood.

For years the only place of worship in Matfen was the Nonconformist chapel. Finally Sir Edward Blackett, tired, it is said, of the invidious comparisons that were constantly being made, erected a church in the Early English style, complete with a spire that unintentionally lends a note of levity to an outstandingly decorous village. In point of fact most of the place only dates back, like the church, to the mid-nineteenth century when West Matfen, as it was then known, was remodelled as an estate village. The result, nevertheless, is very pleasant, with the Hall in the background, a sufficiency of trees and then a village green with a well-executed war memorial in the form of a Celtic cross. The green itself is much enhanced by the stone-lined channel which, like a miniature canal, carried the water from Catcleugh on its way to the Whittledene Reservoirs at Harlow Hill.

A little to the south a number of grass mounds are all that is left of the medieval village of East Matfen, which tradition insists was decimated by the plague. On the way lies the queer castellated farmhouse of Standing Stone with, opposite it, the seven-foot 'menhir' that gives the place its name. Inscribed with the cup-and-ring markings that have proved such a puzzle to archaeologists, it shows evidence that the cracks caused by extremes of temperature and subsequent rainfall have been used by the villagers for sharpening their swords. Since then, no doubt, as Wilfrid Gibson, the Hexham poet, put it:

> The sarsen stone
> Doorpost of temple, altar—throne
> Of some old god, or monument
> Erected by a warrior host
> To mark the fallen chieftain's tomb
> In course of time has come
> To serve the old black sow for scratching post.

West of Matfen lies Great Whittington—a pleasant if undistinguished village very typical of the Tyne valley. There is no church, however, but a Methodist chapel originally financed (like the Congregational church at Horsley) by the rent from a neighbouring farm which was therefore known as the Whiggs. In the middle of the village is to be found a considerable agricultural engineering business, while at the lower end stands a little inn, the 'Queen's Head'. Its entrance passage is decorated with a series of murals showing Dick Whittington entering London, then talking to a number of what look like Red Indians, and finally in the robes of Lord Mayor. Someone must presumably have thought there was a connection.

From Great Whittington (Little Whittington is but a farm) the way north lies upwards along what once formed part of the Devil's Causeway, known hereabouts (after one of the ancient 'yetuns' or giants who frequented these parts) as Cobb's Causeway. On the windswept brow of the hill lies the tiny hamlet of Ryal—the Rye Hill—consisting of a small church, two or three farms and virtually nothing else.

Fighting your way past an apparently endless stream of lorries filled with road-stone from the Moat Law quarries that border the ancient Carrier's Way, you approach another of the tiny hamlets that grace this part of the world. This is Ingoe, the Heugh or Spur of a hill where Inga lived, and no name could be more apt, for it sticks up above the surrounding countryside rather like an Italian mountain village.

It is a curious little place, approached by a few yards of steep hill from the Kirkheaton road, and consisting of a number of single-storey stone houses that were originally built for the pitmen working the tiny collieries that are now no more. Its austerity, however, is lessened by some modern bungalows, while a quarter of a mile away stands Ingoe Hall with its pleasant stone-slab roof.

This is almost moorland country, some seven hundred feet above sea level, on which graze hill sheep and hardy cattle, rather than the fatteners down below, and where the villages—Kirkheaton, Great Bavington, Hallington—are little larger than Ryal or Ingoe. One's first impression of Kirkheaton is one of isolation, which perhaps is not surprising considering that the road finishes here! Right on the 750-foot contour, and built round a large green, it is another quaint little place, with an equally quaint little church that stands almost at the top of the hill on which the village is built, and is approached by a grass path. Originally known as Little Heaton, the High Town (for that is what Heaton means) owes much of its attraction to a splendid seventeenth-century manor house, where Oliver Cromwell is reputed to have stayed, and which includes part of the bastle that preceded it. The estate, however, of which the village formed part, has had a pretty stormy history. In 1296 it was shown as one of the possessions of Hexham Priory; since when Middletons, Ildertons, Swinburnes, Herons, Bewicks, Crasters, Stotes, have all quarrelled over it.

Some four miles away lies the other Heaton, which used to be distinguished from its neighbour by being known as Magna or Caput (Head) Heaton. Standing just off the Newcastle-to-Jedburgh road, Capheaton is approached by Silver Lane, so called from the discovery there of a number of Roman coins and a service of Roman plate, dug up about the time of the Forty-five and now in the British Museum. It is a tiny estate village, consisting of a single terrace of houses with a delightful view, built as were so many Northumberland villages, in the eighteenth century, in order to replace the hovels of the past. In medieval times there was a castle here, which was "moated about and had a drawbridge and was a place of resort in the mosstrooping times".

It was in 1668 that that consummate architect Robert Trollop contracted "to build for Sir John Swinburne of Capheaton, baronet, one new house at Capheaton, which shall be in length eight and twenty yards and in breadth twenty yards from outside to outside . . . in consideration of the sum of £500," and created what Pevsner has described as "one of the most interesting houses of its date and character in England". The grounds were landscaped, and the lake designed, by Capability Brown.

When King Oswald fought and defeated the heathen Cadwallon, it was near Hallington (the Holy Dene) that the contest, afterwards known as the Battle of Heavenfield, took place. Apart from its reservoir, this must be the village's only claim to fame for, with the exception of an eighteenth-century hall that overlooks a delightful wooded dene, there is little else of note.

From Hallington the road climbs gently northward to Little Bavington; then on to a bare whinstone plateau eight hundred feet in height, where, apparently in the middle of nowhere, lies its larger neighbour, where Babba's people also had a homestead. In his *History of Northumberland* the Reverend John Hodgson wrote of Great Bavington 150 years ago as consisting of a farmhouse and a few cottages, but thought that there had once been a mill there and that the place was "formerly much more extensive". Since his day this oasis in a particularly bare countryside does not seem to have changed a lot, but what it lacks in size it makes up in interest, at any rate to Presbyterians.

From the time that William Veitch, the famous Covenanter, sought refuge in Northumberland in 1672, his teachings found a ready response among a notably dour population, and soon there were congregations not only in the extreme north of the county but at Fallowlees (where Veitch made his home for some years), at Belsay, at North Middleton and at Great Bavington itself. There is some evidence that services were being held at Ladywell, a farm just to the north of the village, even before Veitch appeared on the scene, and certainly the Communion Cups in use in the church are Cromwellian. Soon the congregation had increased to 300, a number quite startling in such a sparsely populated area; particularly as it included no less than twelve county voters.

In 1725 the present church was completed, but in 1801 a crisis developed on the death of the Reverend James Rutherford, the congregation failing to agree on a new minister. The battle continued to rage until November 1802 when the two parties agreed to differ. The majority continued to worship in the church at Great Bavington; the minority in the manse and subsequently in a barn in the neighbouring village of North Middleton, where we shall meet them again.

Since then a new manse has been built, the intention being to turn the old one "into a school-house and master's house and to make the Institution of such a character as should induce the wealthy farmers and graziers of the neighbourhood to send their children to it instead of sending them to boarding school to finish their education". It was a praiseworthy object, but perhaps over-optimistic in the case of an isolated spot like Great Bavington. The school and the master's house have now been joined together, modernized and divided again into two.

Across to the Jedburgh road, and just before one begins the long climb to the moors known as the Ottercops there nestles on the bank of the Wansbeck another *tun*, or homestead, this time created by the Followers of someone nicknamed the Whelp or Cub. This, in fact, is Kirkwhelpington. Its neighbour, from which it was originally differentiated by the presence of a church, was more recently known as West Whelpington, and it was much the more important of the two. Subsequently its prosperity declined and early in the eighteenth century it disappeared altogether, leaving only the ghostly remains in the turf to show where a village dating back to the eleventh century had once been.

By the standards of the district in which it finds itself, K.W.

(as the inhabitants call it) is surprisingly large, and beautifully kept. Obviously the Parish Council is proud of its heritage, and the place boasts some of the tidiest village greens (there are more than one) and one of the best-equipped halls, in the county. It is also apparently very healthy, for that great antiquarian the Reverend Anthony Hedley, who was curate here in the early days of the eighteenth century, calculated that (even in those days) one in every six-and-a-half of his parishioners lived to be over eighty. What happened to the other half he did not say.

Weekenders seem conspicuous here by their absence, but it is no surprise to find that a number of people have found Kirkwhelpington sufficiently attractive to convert old buildings into modern dwelling houses; among them the Temperance Hotel and the Mill House. The fulling mill no longer exists, though its name is perpetuated by Walk Mill Farm. Two main streets, and one or two subsidiary ones, accommodate not only the older stone houses but a delightful building known as the Courthouse, which used to serve as a police station, and a number of comparatively inoffensive council houses.

St Bartholomew's church, with its handsome, squat tower, is interesting because it remains typical of the older Northumbrian churches as they were originally built, that is to say, long and narrow with tower, nave and chancel but no transepts. Mostly thirteenth century, if not earlier, the length of the nave and chancel together (but excluding the tower) is 102 feet, but its greatest breadth only 20 feet. There is a memorial to Sir Charles Parsons, the distinguished inventor and scientist and creator of the steam turbine, who lived at nearby Ray Demesne, and is buried in the churchyard here.

The vicarage, built in the middle of the eighteenth century, is notable not only for its intriguing appearance but for the fact that it was here that the Reverend John Hodgson, when he was vicar, wrote the greater part of his immensely erudite work, the *History of Northumberland*, which he was never able to finish, but which has since been supplemented by no less than fifteen volumes published by a committee created for the purpose.

Within a few miles of Kirkwhelpington there stand three great houses whose owners, the Swinburnes of Capheaton, the Loraines of Kirkharle and the Fenwicks, Blacketts and Trevelyans of Wallington, have exerted at one time or another, an overmastering influence over this part of Northumberland. The Wallington estate was presented by the late Sir Charles Trevelyan to the nation and is now looked after by the National Trust. With it went the magnificent Hall and the estate village of Cambo, once the Spur with a Crest. And a very apt description it is, with the tree-girt church standing up as a landmark for miles around and the village itself looking down over the wide valley of the Wansbeck.

Wallington Hall is one of the show places of Northumberland and as such is a lily that hardly needs gilding. Nor, seeing that it stands more than a mile from the village, need it concern us here. On the other hand Cambo has never really received the acclaim that it deserves. As a model village it rivals Blanchland and, for my money, altogether eclipses its competitors in the north of the county—namely Ford and Etal. Begun by Sir Walter Blackett in the middle of the eighteenth century, that golden age for estate villages (and for great mansions as well), and added to later, it is laid out in terraces grouped within the corner made by two roads. Shielded almost entirely from both, it conveys an astonishing feeling of peace and seclusion, and with its houses of warm stone, and gardens in which the villagers seem to vie with each other to produce the most colourful displays, it is something of a showpiece.

Perhaps the pleasantest part of a notably attractive village is the southernmost terrace, with its fine view and the two larger houses at the ends, one of which was originally the agent's, while that at the west corner used to be a pub. Known as the 'Two Queens', it still bore, not so long ago, a sign showing Elizabeth I on one side, Mary Queen of Scots on the other. The post office-cum-village-shop has been converted from a small Border tower, and in the middle of the village is a *pant*—that is to say, a drinking fountain —on which is carved a most ferocious-looking dolphin and the curiously ironic words "Not unmindful of future generations". Ironic because they are in Latin, and it is precisely those future generations that are unlikely to understand them.

It was at Cambo that Lancelot Brown obtained any schooling he had. Born in 1716 on the Kirkharle estate, he started work there as garden boy, and subsequently became gardener, to Sir William Loraine, for whom he laid out the park. It was the great age of landscape gardening and after some seven years he went to work for Lord Cobham at Stowe. Later he designed gardens for the highest in the land, and his habit of remarking that "this place has great capabilities" earned him the title of Capability Brown. So famous did he become as the designer of such gardens as Blenheim, Richmond and Kew that he was able to marry Sir William Loraine's daughter and become, of all things, High Sheriff for the counties of Huntingdon and Cambridge.

Here in Cambo there lived (at much the same time) Thomas Whittle, the author of "The Mitford Galloway's Ramble" and other dialect poems, and the eccentric schoolmaster William Robson, himself a satirist, who published Whittle's poems and kept for twenty-three years a rhyming register of the children who attended his school.

> The names distinguished by a star
> Were the most docible by far:
> And those with equi-distant strokes
> Were second-handed sort of folks;
> But where you find the letter B
> A humdrum booby you will see;
> And where an exclamation's set,
> The rascals went away in debt.

From Cambo it is no great distance to the tiny, tree-lined hamlet of Middleton. Once a much larger place, it is believed to have formed part of the estates of King Malcolm of Scotland. When Arkle Morell, the steward and kinsman of Robert Mowbray, Earl of Northumberland, slew Malcolm in the latter's attack on Alnwick, he is thought to have been awarded Middleton in recognition of his deed. As Middle Town is a fairly common name in Northumberland, as elsewhere, the place was known for long enough as Middleton Morell to distinguish it from the others. Later on it was called North Middleton so as to avoid confusion with another village a mile or two to the south, where now only a farmstead remains. Losing much of its importance over the years, North Middleton now consists only of the Hall, a few houses and the United Reformed church that was built in 1816 by the seceding congregation of Great Bavington, and known accordingly as the United Secession.

Before proceeding to the delights of Hartburn, one should really refer to Belsay, which has so far, for reasons of geography, been ignored. Here we have another Spur in the shape of the Heugh where Bill (a diminutive of Bilheard) once lived. Since the twelfth century the estate has been in the hands of one family—the Middletons—albeit that at different times they have taken the name of Lambert and, in the nineteenth century, of Monck. One of them, Sir Gilbert Middleton, created a considerable stir when, quarrelling with Edward II, he raised a private army of Borderers, ravaged Northumberland and Durham, seized a couple of cardinals from Rome and the Prince Bishop of Durham whom they were about to induct, and squeezed out of them a considerable ransom. In the end, however, Edward caught up with him: he was executed and his lands were confiscated, only to be returned later on to the family.

The residence from which the egregious Gilbert, or at any rate his descendants, operated was what has been described as "by far the most imposing specimen of castellated architecture in North-umberland," in the form of an L-shaped tower. In 1614 a wing was added in which the family could live more comfortably. The tower still stands in a remarkably complete state, but the wing, though it is not so long since it was occupied, is now falling into disrepair.

Early in the nineteenth century that pillar of the Whig Aris-tocracy and Member of Parliament for Northumberland, Sir Charles Monck (who had changed his name from Middleton in 1799) assumed the mantle of an improving landlord that had proved so attractive to others. It was while spending his honey-moon in Athens that Sir Charles fell under the spell of Greek architecture. Returning, he sought out young John Dobson, then almost unknown, and together they produced Belsay Hall, with its immense fluted columns like a Greek temple, using the warm brown stone from a quarry on the estate.

In the process of building the Hall (now unfortunately empty) and its gardens, Sir Charles demolished the old village of Belsey, and rebuilt it some distance to the east, where it stands today. A tiny estate village, it consists mainly of a terrace of houses (arcaded this time in the Italian style) plus a school which it dated 1841. The erstwhile pub, of roughly the same date, is now known as 'Wood House'.

From Belsay it is but a little way to the Homestead on the Arched Hill, in other words Whalton. Originally a village of bastle houses designed to withstand attack by the Scots, and by any reivers who might take a fancy to the villagers' cattle, it once belonged to the Lords Scrope, two of whom were Wardens of the West March. Now the bastles have disappeared in favour of a wide, tree-lined street with a pleasant grass bank to the north, where stand a number of surprisingly large houses, while to the south the cottage gardens lend colour to a delightful scene. At the west end is a fine pub, the 'Beresford Arms', the name of which is a reminder that one of the considerable landowners in these parts is Lord Decies, whose family inherited land once belonging to the Delavals. Near the east end stands the Manor House. This is something of a misnomer, in the sense that it is comparatively modern. It is in fact the outcome of a very successful conversion by Sir Edwin Lutyens of four cottages that had already been somewhat enlarged. The wings have not been greatly altered, but inside the entrance the upper and lower hall and a circular dining-room help to draw the house together. The whole is in a sense typical of Whalton which, only six miles from Morpeth and fifteen from Newcastle, has proved a very pleasant refuge not only for the retired but for business people as well.

The church contains a good deal of thirteenth-century work, while the tower is Norman, though rather spoilt by a neo-Gothic top. Within the rectory are two vaulted basements and the remains of a circurlar staircase, that show there was once a vicar's peel here. No doubt the inhabitants of the United States would claim that the fourth of July was their own invention, but Whalton got there first, for on that date the villagers have lighted, since time immemorial, a bale fire on the green for the children to dance round, though they no longer go the whole hog by jumping through the flames.

There is no need to pause for long at Meldon—the Hill where a Cross, or some other monument, once stood. Though writ large on the ordnance map it consists of nothing much more than a farm or two, the church, the kennels of the Morpeth Hunt and the quaint little Deer Keeper's house. A mile away to the north stands a fine old country pub called 'The Dyke Neuk'.

Hartburn, however, is a very different kettle of fish. As you approach it from the east, beware of the sharp turn over the Hart Burn that lies at the bottom of the wooded hill. Once you have negotiated it, however, you will find a most endearing little village. The first point of interest is the church of St Andrew, built in the twelfth and thirteenth centuries and one of the most interesting in the county. With its low, blocky tower, its massive simplicity and the aura of ancient peace that it wears, it is the epitome of a Northumbrian church. Look for the leaning pillar with the fish carved on it, the Cromwellian money chest, the stone coffins and the old gravestones in the churchyard with their skull and cross-bones, or crossed spades. The Knights Templar owned land here-abouts. Hence the 'Knights Templars' Doorway' and their mason marks still to be seen on stones in the church.

Among the graves in the churchyard is that of the Reverend John Hodgson, for many years vicar of Hartburn after leaving Kirkwhelpington; and next door stands the spacious vicarage in which he wrote the latter part of his *History*. Not far from the house runs the Herpeth (or Military Road) as the Devil's Cause-way is known here, though there are no longer any signs of the Roman bridge that once carried it over the Hart Burn.

The village itself consists of a small collection of pretty little stone houses sheltered by trees, and culminating at the west end in the curious School House. This was built in the shape of a tower with a castellated face and a rather unpleasant arched window, by that energetic cleric, Archdeacon Sharpe, when he was vicar here in the latter years of the eighteenth century. The upper part orig-inally acted as the schoolmaster's quarters and the lower as the parish stable. Now it is occupied by the Director of Music to the County Council, whose instruments are housed in what was once the school.

No doubt in years gone by anyone travelling from Hartburn to Netherwitton would have done so along the Devil's Causeway but, since the virtual disappearance of the Roman road, the most direct way has been through the lands that once belonged to the Knights Templar; then through Old Park Wood along a road known for some obscure reason as the Trench. Witton by the Waters, as the place used to be known, must have taken its name of the Wood Town from the forest of which King John later allowed Roger de Merlay to make a park. Finally it became the

The peel tower in Ninebanks

Knarsdale Hall

(*above*) The bier house at Chollerton

(*left*) The Walk Mill tombstone at Chollerton

Otterburn Woollen Mill

Stonehaugh, a forestry village

Ponteland:
the Black-
bird Inn

Stamfordham: the village green

Cambo, an estate village

(*left*) The vicar's peel at Elsdon

(*below*) Once a peel tower, now Cambo Post Office

The manor house at Whalton

The Old Mill at Netherwitton

(*top*) Earsdon: the back lonnen

(*bottom*) The manor house at Mitford

Nether, or Low, Wood Town to differentiate it from Long Witton. "To this day," wrote Hodgson, for once sacrificing literacy to enthusiasm, "the valley of Netherwitton is in its retirement and the extent of its woods, the most unique in Northumberland."

This is very much of an estate village, but nothing like so regimented as most, perhaps because of its position at the meeting of the Ewesley Burn with the Font, which gives it a pleasantly haphazard air. There is no pub here, the original inn having been turned into a post office, though it still retains in front of it, its mounting block, known of course as the 'loupin-on styen'. Where the village green used to be, opposite Font House, stands the old market cross dating from 1698 (though it has since been restored) round which the villagers used to dance to the music of the Northumbrian pipes. It is a relic of the days when Netherwitton was quite an important place, with its own market, the original village lying to the east of the bridge. Here there still stands the old three-storey corn mill of the manor which, when enlarged in 1794 and supplied with the necessary machinery, manufactured cotton, finally ending up as a woollen mill. Some way behind it is to be found a little church which has taken the place of a much more ancient one. Here, in 1633 a certain Mungo Barnes was charged with laying violent hands on the curate, and was duly excommunicated. No doubt he was much provoked, for it was not long after that the same curate (Mr Andrew Hall) was assaulted by another villager, Thomas Swan.

It is surprising that Great Whittington should have wanted to claim a connection with a Lord Mayor of London when Northumberland in general, and the manor of Witton in particular, once produced his counterpart. This was Roger Thornton, born at the place of that name near Hartburn, who made his fortune in the fourteenth century and finished up as three times mayor of Newcastle. The rhyme about him that is usually quoted runs,

> At the West Gate came Thornton in
> With a hap and a halfpenny in a ram's skin.

though there are at least six other versions. Presumably the halfpenny and the ram's skin were the original capital on which he founded his fortunes as a merchant prince and subsequent Member of Parliament. It is the first word which has sparked off so

G

much argument. In Northumberland we call any kind of covering, from a tarpaulin to a greatcoat, a 'hap', and the natural assumption would be that it was some article of clothing that Roger Thornton had with him. But the word can also mean luck (as in 'mishap') and the Scots have a proverb, "Hap and a halfpenny is warld's gear enough".

Anyway, whether it was luck or perseverance, or whatever, Thornton made a lot of money and built Netherwitton Castle, which is now defunct, though one of its stones, bearing the arms of Thornton and a Latin inscrption reading "In the year of Edward the Fifth", survives above the door in the north front of Netherwitton Hall.

Like Netherwitton, Mitford seems to have had scant respect for its clergy and, at one time during the sixteenth century, the vicar failed to appear altogether, leaving his parish to "a Scotch priest". No doubt he was wise to do so, for in 1570 the parson was subjected to all sorts of indignities. These culminated in his own churchwarden, Gavin Lawson, shouting to him, when he was preaching, to "come down and leave thy prattling," which proved to be the signal for the whole congregation to start a riot. On Easter Day Lawson and others once more made so much noise that they were summoned before the Ecclesiastical Court. "It was a very cold year" explained the churchwarden blandly, "and many one there troubled with the hoose* which was so farvent that many other smiled and laughed thereat." On a further occasion of the same kind the Court came to the conclusion that they must really stand behind the unfortunate vicar, and they excommunicated the culprit.

But all this is getting ahead of the game, for it is not its inhabitants so much as the village itself we should be talking about. The Mythe or Meeting Ford, so called because here the Font meets the Wansbeck, was once an important place.

> Midford was Midford ere Morpeth was ane
> And still shall be Midford when Morpeth is gane.

It is no longer a place of particular note except for its historical associations, but nestling as it does in the wooded valley where,

---

* Cough.

as Swinburne has it, "The Wansbeck sings with all her springs,"
it remains a lovely one.

Approached down the hill from Hartburn it appears as just a
minute village of stone houses, augmented by the small council
estate which is built round a kind of village green. No longer are
there any signs of the factory that once made flannel and then
(of all things) snuff. Nor of the old 'Plough Inn', destroyed by fire
in 1929 and replaced by a new one more famous for its cheese-
and-onion sandwiches than for politics. Here it was, however,
that in 1874 the first stirrings of trade-unionism among the farm
workers (or hinds as they have always been known) were heard in
the county. Stirring is the word, for the chairman addressed the
meeting in rhymed couplets comparing the hinds to the heroes of
mythology, which were greeted with rapturous applause.

Take the road southwards over the Wansbeck and it is a different matter. Here among the trees are a number of expensive-
looking houses, followed by a delightful small vicarage which has
taken the place, and used much of the stone, of a less manageable
one. St Mary Magdalene's (thirteenth-century but much rebuilt)
has a fine spire and it is not Mitford's fault if I find such flights
of fancy out of place in Northumberland. In it there is a crude
effigy of Bertram Reveley of Throphill, bearing the slightly ambigu-
ous inscription:

> Bartram to us so dutiful a son,
> If more were fit it should for thee be done
> Who deceased the 7th of October, Anno Domini 1622.

Fine though the church is, it is the castle, or what is left, that
really steals the show, if only because of the history that attaches
to it. One of William the Conqueror's knights, Sir Richard Bertram, founded a dynasty which, besides endowing Brinkburn
Priory and making numerous other bequests to the church, built
the castle on its lofty motte overlooking the Wansbeck in 1170.
Protected on three sides by the loop of the river that acted as a
moat and gave South Bridge its old name of the Fouse or Fosse
Bridge, its capture must have posed quite a problem. Yet captured
it was in the year of Magna Carta by King John's Flemish troops.
In the following year it withstood the attack of Alexander II of
Scotland, but in 1316 the adventurous Gilbert de Middleton, who

had so recently kidnapped the cardinals, failed to hold it against Edward II. Two years afterwards, Alexander III captured the castle and successfully dismantled it. Now there only remain the ruins of the keep and a little of the outer bailey wall.

The Mitford family entered into possession in the reign of Bloody Mary, and it was not long before they had moved out of what then remained of the castle into a manor house south-west of the church. In 1823, the great John Dobson designed for them Mitford Hall, and they left the manor house to its own devices. Before long, only the kitchen and the entrance tower, bearing the Mitford arms and the date 1637, remained intact. The house was later made into an estate cottage and until quite recently not only the great fireplace but the old dog-spit wheel survived. The latter has since been removed to the Hall, and no longer need a little dog, in order to keep its own balance, endlessly work the tread-mill turning the roast. More recently still, the old house has been turned into one of the most desirable modern residences it is possible to imagine.

Last of the Heartland villages is Longhorsley which, perhaps because of its position astride the Newcastle-to-Coldstream road, is bigger than most, though being built in the shape of a cross the fact is not always apparent to travellers. To the south lies Long-horsley Moor, described by Eneas Mackenzie, when he wrote his *View of the County of Northumberland*, as "the prolific source of contagious disorders incident to cattle, and of little real use in its present state." Since then a good deal has been done to improve the moor and it is to be hoped that the cattle are the better for it. Meanwhile the village has changed somewhat. The old 'Shoulder of Mutton' still caters for travellers, though no longer for the Royal Mail or Wellington coach (four inside), that used to pass this way to and from Scotland; but the 'Rose and Thistle' is now the Rose and Thistle Gallery—perhaps what is now for some reason known as a boutique.

In modern times the village has spread westwards quite con-siderably along the Netherwitton road, and there is a modern school there. Here also stands the Catholic church dedicated to St Thomas of Canterbury and the tower that used at one time to serve the same purpose, and subsequently became the presbytery, but is now a private house. This is the ancient tower of the Horsleys—probably built at some time in the sixteenth century—where Sir Thomas Horsley (rather unwillingly, for he was a Parliamentarian) entertained General Monck and his forces on their way south to effect the Restoration of Charles II. Adjoining the usual vaulted basement is a small room that may well have been used as a prison, while the corkscrew staircase, instead of being in the thickness of the wall, is in an annexe. Four storeys in height altogether, it is a massive affair and, though extensively modernized, retains, unlike most Northumbrian towers, the original battlements.

8

The Southern Coalfield

LUCKY the county that has no warts. Those of Northumberland
are concentrated (perhaps mercifully) in an L-shaped band that
runs as far west as Prudhoe and as far north as Amble—a countryside criss-crossed with wagon-ways and level crossings and dotted
with colliery winding-shafts and spoil-heaps. And with dreary
Victorian villages of red or (low be it spoken) yellow brick terraces
known as 'pit raas', each house with its little back-yard and
'netty', behind which runs the back lonnen that divides one raa
from the next.

But times are changing. The smouldering pitheaps have been
extinguished—some have been removed or contoured into inoffensive hillocks planted with trees and covered with grass. Many
of the pits have been worked out, the buildings partially or totally
dismantled, and the pit raas demolished and replaced by pleasanter houses and bungalows in the modern style. The desolation
of opencast mining has added a new horror to the landscape in
some places but mercifully it does not go on for ever, and the land
is eventually restored, though it may be many years before decent
crops are grown once more. But even this is preferable to the
hundreds, and indeed thousands, of acres which still show the
scars of deep mining in the form of subsidence that has ruined
the drainage and created in many cases 'slacks' and ponds useless
to man or beast. And to the nightmare tangle of pylons and wires
that carry the electricity necessary these days for mining and manu-
facturing, as well as for domestic needs.

To the stranger the villages that the Industrial Revolution has
spawned will no doubt appear uniformly horrible. To appreciate

them at all one must really be steeped in the traditions of the area and of the Geordies who inhabit it. Gone are the days when grimy pitmen in their traditional long-shorts, coloured stockings (known as pit-hoggers) and steel-capped boots, could be seen tramping home to their bath before the kitchen fire, for nowadays they leave the pithead baths looking as normal as anyone else. No longer do they squat on their hunkers* in the dyke-backs† of a Sunday, each with the racing whippet by his side which, even when the rest of the family were on short commons, must still be fed its meat and eggs. Yet the general atmosphere has not greatly altered. A great number of the pit raas still survive, even if they have been provided with amenities undreamt of by an earlier generation. The focal points of the villages—miners' welfare buildings, working men's clubs, the co-operative and the chapel—though flanked with old people's homes and bingo halls—continue to supply the needs of a population who may well prefer them to the buildings and churches that grace our older villages.

It is a scene that changes almost as you watch. As the seams of coal run out, the pits close down and factories spring up to provide jobs for those who have been thrown out of work, to be followed by better houses and opportunities for recreation. It is a new and altogether better world; yet something has been lost where the pits have closed. Mining communities have always been close-knit; held together by a camaraderie inspired by common danger and discomfort, and a respect for hard work, and leavened by a wry humour that has made these villages bearable.

We may as well start as near to Newcastle as possible with the first village that has so far escaped the sprawling connurbation which has already engulfed Westerhope, Denton and Newburn. In point of fact Throckley, that is to say, the Hill where Throc lived (or perhaps the Tumulus where he was buried) no longer belongs to Northumberland. But who cares? Northumbrian such villages have always been, and despite the decisions of commissions and the machinations of civil servants and local authorities, Northumbrian they will surely remain, even if they are now administered by the hermaphrodite council of Tyne-Wear.

* Haunches.
† Hedge-sides.

Throckley is basically a pit-village, for some of the earliest mining in the area took place here. Messrs Bell and Brown, who built Frenchmen's Row at nearby Heddon-on-the-Wall in the last days of the eighteenth century, did so to house their pitmen. Long before then, little shallow mines had been worked all round the village, and there still exist traces of no less than thirty-seven little shafts on three adjoining farms, down which horses, cows and even tractors have disappeared on occasion. Eventually the coal-mining activities of the area were concentrated in two collieries —the Maria and the Isabella. Both have now ceased work, their pitheaps have been reduced or removed and the ground levelled for other purposes, a fate that has also overtaken the old pit raas, whose place has partly been taken by a Catholic church built in the modern idiom.

Just outside the village stands Dewley Farm where George Stephenson, when his father became fireman at the neighbouring colliery, was given his first job by the widow Ainslie. He earned twopence a day for herding her cows on the colliery wagon-way and shutting the farm gates at night. It was not very much, but after all he was only eight, and when he grew old enough to lead the plough horses she doubled his wage.

One of the features of the county is the way in which the water supply for Newcastle and Gateshead is managed. Byrness, Matfen and Hallington are only three of the villages connected with the line of reservoirs—Catcleugh, Sweethope, Colt Crag and Halling-ton—that trap the waters of the Rede and bring them down to the Whittle Dene reservoirs near Horsley. Thence it is by way of the filterbeds at Throckley that the water proceeds to its final destina-tion. Here indeed is a meeting of ancient and modern for when, in 1879, the main pipes were being laid at the Bank Top, a section of the Roman Wall that passes right under the village was brought to light, together with an earthenware vessel in which lay no less than five thousand coins of about A.D. 260.

Skirting the ever-spreading tentacles of Newcastle, and of its airport at Woolsington, one reaches Dinnington,* once a little pit village consisting of a church, chapel, school, a few pitmen's houses and no less than three pubs. More recently the pit has closed

* Which incorporates what was originally known as Mason.

down, but not before considerable developments had taken place. The most ancient of the houses have been razed (including, unfortunately, what was once the communal bakehouse), the farmstead in the middle has disappeared, and in their place are a little village green and an estate of commuter houses. The blacksmith's shop, however, provides continuity to a village that has gained in convenience what it has lost in individuality.

The name Dinnington is thought to signify the Homestead of the People who live on the Hill, and this may well be the case, for it is built on the higher ground below which stretches Prestwick Carr, once a string of lakes frequented by every sort of fowl, but since drained, though with ever-decreasing success, thanks to the disturbance of the levels by mining subsidence. Here it was that in the early days of this century there were discovered a number of copper vessels comprising the cooking equipment which had belonged to a Roman cavalry unit, and may well have been thrown into the water on the occasion of some military 'flap'.

A mile or two to the east lie a number of villages, four of which have virtually grown into each other. The first used to be known as Dinnington Colliery, in order to differentiate it from Dinnington Village. It is only a few years ago that the name was changed —unbelievably—to Brunswick. It would be quite in the tradition of the pit villages that sprung up during the Industrial Revolution that it should be named after foreign victories and victors such as Camperdown, Bomarsund and Blucher. But why, for heaven's sake, Brunswick?

Of all the pit villages in the county it is this place that has changed most radically—and almost all for the better. The 'Ca' Canny' and the 'Travellers' Rest' still quench the thirsts of the inhabitants, though no doubt those thirsts are very different from those of a generation ago. A small industrial estate has taken the place of the colliery, and smart new houses spring up almost overnight.

To the north lies Seaton Burn, another pit village now greatly improved, which takes its name from the burn that fills, and drains, the nearby lake that is now a bird sanctuary. To the north again is Annitsford whose chief, in fact only, claim to distinction lies in its genesis of that great bass, Owen Brannigan, whose success in grand opera, as much as his inimitable rendering of Geordie songs, has caused his birth-place to call one of their streets after him. To the south lies Wideopen, which owes its astonishing name to the wide valley of the burn which eventually reaches the sea at Seaton Sluice.

It was in the middle of the nineteenth century that a village sprang up round the colliery which had been named Hazlerigg after the family who used to own the land. Laid out, like other Victorian pit villages, in red brick terraces, Hazlerigg is another whose appearance has improved out of all recognition since the colliery closed down. Gone now is the spoil-heap that used perpetually to smoulder, giving off a stench that pervaded the countryside for miles around, and in its place has appeared a grass-grown hillock planted with trees. Only one obvious reminder of the past remains in the shape of the wagon-way along which little diesel engines chunter, pulling the coal-laden trucks from the drift nearby that has taken the place of the pitshaft in the village.

Killingworth, the enclosure or homestead where Cylla's People once lived, lies to the north of the coast road through West Moor, where, on the roadside, still stands the cottage where Stephenson lived when he was designing his first locomotives.

Within yards of leaving the main road you find yourself in a leafy lane which finally turns into the village street of Old Killingworth itself—a backwater as different from the utilitarian brick of West Moor as chalk from cheese. On one side of the road stand some pleasant houses, a few of them looking somewhat embarrassed (unless, of course you like that sort of thing) by two absurdly castellated villas. Opposite is the nice old stone farmhouse of Killingworth North Farm, dated 1755, and on the same side of the road the really astonishing church with its attendant church hall, built in the same style. Nikolaus Pevsner, in his "Buildings of England" series, mentions its "polygonal apse", its lack of any tower or belfry, and the fact that it is "built of stones of deliberately varied colour and with bands of red sandstone." What he does not set out to convey is the sense of shock that the casual visitor is likely to experience on being confronted with it without warning. Partly obscured by the trees that literally cover an immense graveyard, the church, with its astonishing mottled appearance and its air of enormous solidity, looks more like some freak of the military, rather than the ecclesiastical, art: in short it is more like a fortress than a church.

One of Northumberland's naval heroes, Admiral Roddam, once lived at Old Killingworth and it is still worth a visit, if only to contrast it with what lies around. It is in fact a bit of an oasis that is only partially insulated from the horrors of Killingworth Township. This is the new town designed to provide 'successful living' for 20,000 of the overspill from Newcastle and elsewhere, but looking more like an army camp surmounted by a prison.

It is no great distance from Cylla's Enclosure to Bacca's—in other words Backworth. We are now entering rather more open country, with heavy crops of wheat competing with the electricity pylons. The first one sees of the village is a vast estate of red-roofed houses, no doubt connected with the new factories to be found in the vicinity. Then comes the old part, in the typical blackened stone of this part of the county, where, until the electrification of pits and the invention of smokeless zones, the soot in the air used, after only a few hours, to leave collars and handkerchiefs a delicate shade of grey. There is no village green here, but the wide, mown verges, and the way in which the houses are set back from the road, give very much the same impression At the east end one comes on the Victorian additions to the village, clustered round the tall winding-shaft of Eccles Colliery, but more or less between the two lie the grounds of Backworth House. This was built in 1780 for Ralph Grey, an ancestor of Lord Grey of Fallodon, by William Newton. It now forms one of the finest miners' recreational centres in the kingdom, while doubling as the clubhouse for the golf-course that goes with it.

It was at Backworth, of all unlikely places, that in the year 1811 there was dug up an astonishing hoard of Roman articles in gold and silver, which eventually found its way to the British Museum. It is thought that it must have been stolen from some settlement on the Roman Wall and buried here by someone who never lived to retrieve it. A mixture of Celtic and Roman design, the hoard consisted of almost new objects that included a silver cooking pot with an elaborate gilt handle, five gold rings, small silver spoons, a brooch in the shape of a harp, gold chains and nearly 300 coins dated A.D. 139 or earlier.

Travelling eastwards, one passes the village school, now a Drama

Centre, and then along a winding road that criss-crosses colliery railways replete with level crossings, guarded and unguarded, and commands to 'whistle here'. It is easy to get lost in these parts, for the whole area is a maze of pits, with their attendant buildings sandwiched between farmsteads and clumps of pitmen's houses, without any very clear signposting. Eventually, however, one reaches Earsdon and the relative safety of main roads.

Eanred or Eored, or whatever his name was, chose well when he picked this Hill for his dwelling. Two and a half miles from the sea, it commands the neighbouring countryside, and the church, with its curiously ornamented tower, can be seen for miles in any direction. It contains, incidentally, some Flemish glass removed from Hampton Court when the latter was being restored. The coats of arms, the supporting greyhound and bear and the Tudor roses, glow as brightly as ever. In the churchyard stands an obelisk in memory of the accident at the Hartley New Pit, one of the worst in history, which took place on 16th January 1862. Over the shaft stretched the beam of the most powerful pumping-engine then known in the north. As the outgoing shift was being drawn up by the winding engine, the forty-ton beam broke and, falling, met the cage coming up, and the whole went down the shaft together, taking a great deal of the timberwork of the shaft with it, so that the mine was blocked, leaving 215 men and boys slowly to suffocate.

Despite the presence of pits all round it, Earsdon remains a largely Georgian village. No longer can the sword-dancers perform their antics on the village green, for it has been lost in the course of widening the main road; but there remain a nice old house, known as the Garth, and a fine Georgian one in the middle of the main street, now occupied by the Water Company. Behind the main street, moreover, and running up to the vicarage, stretches a delightful back lonnen of old grey cottages.

It was at Earsdon, by the way, that in the year 1773 "a Mr Davison, appearing dead, lay as a corpse two days, when the funeral was put off until the third day, in consequence of the absence of a relation; in this interval Mr D. revived, and in a few days was quite well." Lucky Mr Davison!

North of Earsdon the colleries are not quite so thick on the ground, and the countryside becomes more typical of the 'mixed economy' that prevailed until quite recently in South Northumberland. When wages were proportionately lower, and there was far less mechanization on farms, there existed a kind of mutual understanding between those who dug coal and those who ploughed fields; the pitmen forming an integral part of the rural scene. In haytime and harvest they found variation and a useful addition to their beer-money in helping the farmers who, in turn, relied very largely on their assistance.

Down then to the pleasant wooded dene of the Seaton burn and up the other side to Holywell, which takes its name from a number of healing wells, the best known being one dedicated to St Mary. A triangular kind of village, straggling along the road towards Seaton Delaval, and finally deteriorating into pit raas of red or yellow brick, its most attractive feature is the Strother Farm. In the Middle Ages a daughter of one of the Del Strothers, Lords of Lyham (near Wooler) married a Delaval, and this may well have been the reason for connecting their name with a place that belonged for so many years to the latter family. Sometimes known as Old Hall, it is built of the roughly dressed stone which lends such an air to old Northumberland, while the farmhouse still retains its stone-slab roof and mullioned windows, set off by a walled garden with fat gateposts reminiscent of the erstwhile Michelin advertisements.

In Northumberland, Norman families were few and far between, and what there were, such as the Tailbois and Umfravilles, have left hardly a trace of their existence in the names of our villages. Not for us such euphonious names as Coatham Mundeville, Sutton Courtenay or Stanstead Mountfitchet. With one exception: the Homestead by the Sea that for long enough has been connected with the family that followed the Conqueror from Laval. In view of its name it is a little confusing to find that the village of Seaton Delaval lies a good two miles from the sea; the explanation being that the home of the Delavals came first and the pit village that arrived centuries later was named after it.

It is tempting to ignore the place and pass quickly on, as so many others have done, to the glories of Seaton Delaval Hall. Yet the village has a certain interest, for it was one of the original centres of the co-operative movement in Northumberland. It was actually at Cramlington, a couple of miles to the west, that the movement began. The colliery owners and companies had for long enough kept 'tuck-shops' at each pit, from which the pitmen were virtually forced to buy their requirements, and it was in desperation at the exorbitant prices charged that they conceived the idea of clubbing together to send one of their number into Newcastle to buy what they needed in bulk. Anyone who cares to take a closer look at Seaton Delaval is likely to be struck by a conglomeration of gloomy-looking red brick buildings that surround a large yard near the centre of the village, and to look for an explanation. In fact this is all that remains of the central warehouse, offices and stables of the Co-operative Society which developed out of these tentative beginnings.

Right on the coast lies Hartley, originally the Hill where Stags were to be found, but later famed for its salt pans. Here it was that the Delavals of Delaval Hall erected a glassworks. As their trade in salt, glass and above all coal increased, they found that the tiny harbour at the mouth of the Seaton burn was not deep enough for the vessels which handled it. Accordingly in 1670 Sir Ralph Delaval constructed a sluice (some of whose stonework still remains near the present road bridge) with gates that opened and shut with the tide, so that the pent-up waters of the burn could be released with enough force to shift the sand which threatened to silt up the harbour. About a hundred years later Sir John Hussey Delaval went a step further by making a cut in the solid rock 300 yards long, 30 wide and 50 feet deep, to carry the water out in a straight line instead of allowing it to wander out by the original channel.

Hartley itself now consists partly of terraces of typical seaside houses that line the old coast road and overlook the lighthouse of St Mary's Island, and partly of a residential estate built a little further inland. It was in the centre of the village here that there used to stand a stone weighing fifteen hundredweight that William Carr, the strong man of Blyth, was supposed to have lifted. Six feet four inches in height and weighing twenty-four stone, he is reputed to have carried a ten-hundredweight anchor to his father's smithy for repair, and to have leapt over a five-barred gate with an eight-stone girl under his arm.

It is difficult to disentangle Hartley from Seaton Sluice. The latter really consists of the harbour, a few houses lining a kind of triangular village green, and a couple of pubs, the King's Arms on top of the cliff, and a little further inland the baroque bulk of the Waterford Arms.

South of Hartley lie Whitley Bay and the whole connurbation of Tyneside, so that it is now a matter of returning through Seaton Delaval to Seghill. Here the closure of the pit has led to a rapid transformation, including the provision of modern houses and the contouring and grassing over of the pitheap. A number of unfortunate yellow brick houses and, of course, the Social Club, are virtually all that is left to remind one of the past.

Of Burradon, the epitome of the pit village, surrounded as it is by collieries, there is little to report unless one takes the lane to Burradon Farm where there stands, almost hidden by sycamores, the remains of an old Border tower, of which only the north wall and the traditional barrel-vaulted 'basement' remain intact. Built sometime in the sixteenth century, it may well have succeeded some much earlier building that gave the place its name of the Hill with a *burh* or Fortified Place on it.

Next door to Burradon lies Camperdown, which was presumably renamed in honour of the battle of 1797, but which had previously been known as Hazlerigg, a designation subsequently transferred to the Victorian village that now bears the name. The centre of Camperdown is, rather surprisingly, embellished with a striking crescent of Old People's Homes, built in a dark red brick with red-tiled roofs. In front are a low brick wall, trees and rose beds, and in the centre the club to which the inhabitants can repair for entertainment. The whole provides a shining example of what can be done with a little imagination even in the most dreary surroundings.

Of Dudley there is little to say except that it is improving, while its brand new suburb of Fordley consists of a residential estate for those working in the light industries that are appearing all around.

Since Cramlington took its name (it is thought) from the Cranes' Spring, it has undergone many vicissitudes, including a considerable increase in size with the nineteenth-century expansion in coal mining. For many years an airship hangar nearby provided a landmark which could be seen for miles around, and it was here also that such flying as was carried out in the early days of aeroplanes took place. Recently a great effort has been made in these parts to provide alternative employment for those who would otherwise have been thrown out of work by continual pit closures. Industrial estates, such as those of Bassington, Nelson and Cramlington itself, provide jobs not only for displaced pitmen but for their women folk, while, as at Killingworth, a complete new town has now sprung up. Yet old Cramlington village has somehow managed to retain its individuality. The pits may have closed down, but the Wesleyan church and the Welcome chapel have survived, and the lofty tower of the parish church still dominates the countryside, while opposite the Blagdon Arms the Social Club is as busy as ever. The New Town, unlike Killingworth which is a government venture, owes its inception to the County Council, and is designed to hold 60,000 people "in a country and rural setting". So far the experiment seems reasonably successful, and it is interesting to find how many people living there are anxious to preserve the village atmosphere while still taking advantage of the adjoining new town—even to the extent of founding a Local History Society in order to keep in touch with the past. The Miners' Gala still survives, and has been supplemented by the Cramlington Fair.

Gone, surely, are the bad old days of starvation wages in the pits, and of unemployment there, which led at the time of the General Strike of 1926 to an unfortunate exercise in what we would now call militancy, still remembered in Cramlington. Some pitmen came across a gang of plate-layers on the main line nearby and, accusing them of blacklegging, chased them away and tore up the length of railway line they had been working on. Despite a warning being given by the plate-layers, the *Flying Scotsman* was unable to stop, and left the rails, three carriages overturning. Nine arrests were made and eight of the Cramlington men sent to prison. In these days of bombing and hijacking all this may seem very small beer, but in a more orderly era the derailment brought the village a measure of publicity which it could well have done without.

When the Ancient Britons settled on the shores of the bay that reaches from Blyth up to Newbiggin, and near a bend in the River Blyth, they had good reason to name the place Camus, meaning something crooked. Many hundreds of years later, Norman clerks, in order to suit themselves, spelt it Cambois, but the inhabitants would have none of it. They had always pronounced it Camus, they went on doing so and it is to be hoped that they always will.

But what could those ancients think if they were to return to Cambois today? One's first sight of the place, particularly from a distance, is of the enormous power station with its huge chimneys belching steam, its conveyers and elevators stretching across the very road. For this is the focal point of the network of pylons and cables that criss-cross the countryside for miles around.

Once the province of fishermen and of smugglers, Cambois later turned to the export of grindstones and grain. Now grindstones are no longer needed, and in other ways also the place has drastically changed. Turn right towards the river and you encounter first the grain silos and cranes and other clanjamfry of a dockside; then one of the staithes so typical of the coal trade; in other words an elevated platform to carry the wagon-way to the waterside, where the coal is dropped into the ships' holds. Finally, on the very point of land at which the Blyth flows into the sea, you reach the unloading facilities and silos for the bauxite imported to feed the giant aluminium smelter of Lynemouth.

Back through the network of railway lines and level crossings lies the featureless red brick of Stakeford and Guide Post. These are Victorian colliery villages with, inevitably, their Miners' Welfare Institutes and Social Clubs, their chapels and shops, and their typical terraces of houses, each with its netty (as the pitman calls his outside loo), and the back lonnens behind. Lower down, on the banks of the Wansbeck, lie the building estate and the few older houses that constitute the village of Sheepwash. This is the highest point to which the Tide reaches and to which Ships used to come up the river—hence the name Ship Wash. It might have been otherwise if the citizens of Morpeth had had their way. Anxious to increase their own prosperity, they employed the famous wizard, Michael Scott, to bring the tide up to their town. Muttering the necessary spells, the wizard told a boy that if he ran along the river bank, the tide would follow him; but on no account whatever must he look behind, or all would be lost. When he got as far as Sheepwash, however, the noise of the sea following him caused the boy to look over his shoulder, the spell was broken and the tide turned.

From the ridiculous to the sublime, from the grim uniformity of the pit-villages to the delightful commuter houses of Hepscott. Here we are back in the countryside proper, though within a mile or two of the town of Morpeth. The station, on the main line from London to Edinburgh, is now closed and the station buildings converted into an attractive, if occasionally noisy, dwelling house. Not far away there appears a squat little Victorian church. An excellent example of the bricklayer's art, it nevertheless looks quite out of place where it is, and would perhaps be more at home in New England.

The village itself now consists of a number of modern villas sheltering among the trees, and interspersed at the west end with a few older houses. The latter include a traditional smithy, now mercifully subject to a preservation order, and Hepscott Hall, a jumble of architecture so astonishing as to deserve a few words all to itself.

The front consists of a square stone erection with a flat roof that looks, except for its windows, like a truncated peel tower. Behind it, and only a foot or two higher, appears the lower part of another tower, while to one side is a wing of old brick that appears to have been added on about the end of the seventeenth century. In the older part there are faint traces of what may have been the circular staircase that one would expect in a tower, but the traditional tunnel vaulting appears not in the tower itself but in the annexe adjoining. When the hall first appears in history (in 1603) it is as a tower with a lower tower in front, the two being united by a roof all of the same pitch. It was then part of the estate of Lord William Howard of Naworth, better known as Bauld Willie, or Belted Will. The flat roofs are the result of a recent fire.

The last of our villages in this area of Northumberland is Stannington, which still bestrides the Great North Road as it did when it was known as the Stane-way-ton, the Homestead on the Paved Road. All in all it is rather a disappointing little place. Standing on a hill that slopes down to the River Blyth, the church, with its tall tower, can be seen for miles around, but the village itself promises more than it can perform. With a scattering of stone houses largely connected with the Blagdon estate, it boasts a good modernized pub, a conglomeration of unattractive new houses, and not very much else. It is a sign of the times, or perhaps a gesture of humanity by the powers that be, that a foot-bridge has been erected to take the inhabitants from one part of the village to the other over the teeming traffic of the A1.

9

The Northern Coalfield

O F all the rivers of Northumberland few have inspired as much poetry and praise as the Wansbeck, or with more reason. Rising on the moors—known familiarly as the Wilds of Wannie—which surround the Sweethope Loughs, it ambles gently down through Kirkwhelpington, a little purling stream. At a point just east of Hartburn, however, it is joined by the Hart Burn and, at Mitford, by the Font, after which it attains, in its wooded valley, the full majesty that has inspired such poets as Swinburne and Mark Akenside. With all this loveliness it is a cruel twist of fate that has allowed the lower reaches to run through one of the richest parts of the coalfield.

Both Ashington ("the largest pit village in the world") and Newbiggin-by-the-Sea are for all practical purposes towns, and there is therefore no point in describing them. Once upon a time, like most of the flatter and drier land, this area must have been covered by forest. It would be a mistake, however, to think that this is the origin of the name Pegswood, for until recently it was known as Pegsworth—in other words Peg's Enclosure. I wonder what Peg—whoever he was—would think if, like Rip Van Winkle, he were to return to the place. Endless terraces of red brick houses, the remains of a colliery whose buildings have nearly all been cleared away, a confection of yellow brick that turns out to be the Methodist church, the usual pubs and clubs, and a school that stands in the shadow of an enormous pit-heap—these are Pegswood today.

All is not lost, however, for the descent of a steep hill to the wooded banks of Wansbeck reveals a tiny gem of a village almost hidden away in its own woods, and as different in every way from Pegswood as it is possible to imagine. This is Bothal, the Low Ground by the river where Bota once carved himself a homestead, and a very pleasant homestead it must have been. For centuries the village has belonged to the old Northumbrian family of Ogle; the present owner, the Duke of Portland, being descended from them in the female line. And not only the village but the historic castle which, almost surrounded by some splendid trees, is best viewed from the other side of the Wansbeck, using the stepping-stones so thoughtfully provided. Quite apart from its historic significance, it provides the setting for a number of legends including that of Lady Jean Ogle, who loved an Umfraville of Otterburn, but whose parents were anxious for her to wed Lord Dacre.

> I never lov'd Lord Dacre yet;
> I dinna like him still—
> He kens, though oft he sued for love
> Upon his bended knee,
> Ae tender word, ae kindly look
> He never gat frae me.

In the end the lady, of course, got her way; a bugle-note "not loud but clear" heralding her lover's arrival to bear her away to Otterburn, leaving Lord Dacre, when he discovered what had happened, "dowf and blunkit".* Serves him right!

There now remains little more than the gatehouse, upon which the leaden figures of warriors still endeavour to persuade besieging forces that the garrison is greater than it is. It has been let to an electronics company, who use it as a guest-house, retaining as much of the medieval atmosphere as possible—the Hungerford dining table for instance, which dates back to the Tudors, being used for important guests.

If prizes were given for the pleasantest and best-kept churchyard in the county, one should surely go to St Andrew's at Bothal. Adorned with flowers and flowering shrubs, it graces a fine thirteenth-century church. If there is anything more attractive than a Saxon tower or Norman arch it is the rough, sturdy little bell towers that set off some of our most ancient churches, symbolic

---

* Doleful and disappointed.

of the grim and rugged traditions of Northumberland. St Andrew's boasts not only such a belfry but also some fine medieval stained glass and a marble tomb of about 1512, carved with the figures of Ralph, Lord Ogle, and his wife.

Continuing eastwards it is possible, with care, to reach Lynemouth without becoming entangled in the purlieus of Ashington or Newbiggin. Only to be confronted by a whole complex of chimneys, elevators, conveyors and all the rest of the paraphernalia, not only of the big modern colliery whose seams run out under the North Sea, but of the aluminium smelter it supplies. Built at the end of the nineteen-sixties, the latter has been the subject of a good deal of foreboding lest the fall-out problems which beset similar smelters in Canada and elswhere should be repeated; for the dust, if allowed to escape, can be absorbed by grazing cattle and affect their bone structure. It was only after a guarantee that the most stringent precautions would be observed that the company was finally given the go-ahead.

Lynemouth itself is no seaside village, as one might reasonably expect, but a collection of houses that sprang up between the wars, above the deep ravine of the Lyne, to house the pitmen who worked this most productive of collieries. Since when, of course, it has grown both in size and in quality, in order to cater for those who run the smelter.

Almost touching Lynemouth is the much older village of Ellington; first settled by Ella's People, then adapted to house pitmen at nearby collieries, and finally enlarged to house in pleasant double-garaged villas the top brass of Lynemouth. It is a curious little place, with the pit raas conveniently separated from the older houses, a number of bungalows and a fine pub. In the centre of the village and in the middle of a row of houses moreover, stands a curious little tower known as The Ducket. About sixteen feet square and a bare two storeys in height, it looks almost like a miniature peel tower except for the castellation and the pigeon holes at the top. Was it once a look-out tower or, as its name suggests, a dovecot or, despite its apparently ancient stonework, just a folly? No one seems to know.

A mile or two to the north-east, and some way now from the Stream where Watercress grew and gave Cresswell its name, stands the real thing—a genuine Border tower that dates back to the fourteenth century and is still in a fair state of repair. Perched in the woods near the Ellington road and overlooking the sea, it was built by the Cresswell family, who have been here ever since. Eventually it proved too small (or too stark) for comfort and a manor house was added to it, which in the seventeenth century was replaced with another, but this has also vanished, and the tower remains in solitary grandeur, complete with the familiar vaulted basement and spiral staircase.

Druridge Bay, with its magnificent crescent of sand, is one of the glories of the Northumberland coast, and it is overlooking the flat rocks that adorn its southern end that there stretches the tiny straggling village of Cresswell. Some of the cottages have been converted to house weekenders; others remain as they have for generations, including the present Manor House with its delightful garden. A coastguard station and a St John's Ambulance First Aid Post lend a nautical air to a place that has managed in the face of every sort of temptation to survive largely unspoilt.

Hebron and Tritlington are little more than snug hamlets almost entirely devoted to agriculture, but the Long Wood that we now know as Longhirst is certainly worth a visit. One's first impression is indeed one of a long wood, for trees are everywhere, almost hiding the little modern church with its untypical spire. Nowhere are the trees finer, or more in evidence, than in the park of Longhirst Hall, one of John Dobson's first efforts. Mackenzie, describing the hall in 1825, the year after it was built, writes of "a complete suite of convenient and handsome out-offices" having just been erected. Alas, the hall is now an Approved School for naughty boys, and the handsome out-offices, in other words the stables and estate buildings that surround a courtyard plumb in the middle of the village, have been converted into houses for the masters.

The pub was closed some time ago and it is something of a grievance that the inhabitants are now dependent on neighbouring Ulgham for their beer.

When writing of Cambois, reference might well have been made to the way in which, while the spelling of placenames alters with passing whims, the pronunciation normally survives unchanged. But, just as Cambois is the classic example of this rule, it is the old Owl-wham or Sheltered Corner frequented by Owls, that provides the exception necessary to prove it for, to the utter undoing of strangers to the district, it is pronounced Uffam.

With the closing of nearby pits and the substitution of new industries not far away, the whole character of the village seems to be changing. There remain, for instance, the old stone houses, but these are now supplemented by a number of new ones, the shaft of the old village cross now finding itself wedged into the garden of a brand-new bungalow. And what of the famous Ulgham Oak that, at seven feet above the ground, measured nearly twenty-two feet in circumference? "A most weird, ghostly tree," declared a visitor, "more like a huge druidical stone than a tree: no leaves, no bark, no life!" Now, unfortunately, it has disappeared, and with it the still from which so much do-it-yourself whisky was once produced.

Next stop is a pit village known as Widdrington Station, which is enough to make you "stare and stretch your eyes". Here, as one might expect from the name, is a station on the main Edinburgh line, but also Stobswood colliery and the sidings from which an infinity of coal has been moved over the years. Also, alas, a brickworks originally run in conjunction with that same colliery, which has apparently gone berserk and spawned millions of white bricks, which have found their way not only into the endless pit raas that bear an unfortunate resemblance to the inside of a public lavatory but, heaven help us, a church as well.

Once one has crossed the main line, it is past a countryside restored (more or less) after the depredations of opencast coal-mining that the road approaches Widdrington proper. Since its origin as the Homestead of Wuduhere's people the tiny seaside village has been notable mainly for the Widdrington family and the castle they inhabited. It was, for instance, "a squyar of Northomberlonde, Ric. Wytharynton was his nam" who allegedly fought in the battle of Chevy Chase and

> . . . when both his leggis were hewyne in to,
> Yet he knyled and fought on hys kne.

And it was in the castle here that there lived Sir Robert Carey (who had married the widow of Sir Henry Widdrington) when he was Warden of the Middle March, the man who scooped the news of Elizabeth's death before it was officially announced, and rode hell-for-leather to Edinburgh to inform James VI that he had come into his English inheritance. Here it was, moreover, that James spent his first night after leaving Berwick on the way south. One's first glimpse of Widdrington is the red spire of the little United Reformed church on one side of the road, followed on the other by the lovely twelfth-century church of Holy Trinity. Once a good deal larger than it is now, it stands on the slopes of a rocky knowe from which there rose the famous tower, or castle, of which nothing whatever now remains, except an avenue of lime trees known as the Twelve Apostles.

The village, nestling under the seaward side of the castle hill is small and pleasant. It was in 1691 that Admiral Sir Ralph Delaval, the builder of Seaton Delaval Hall, succeeded in blockading in Dunkirk harbour a French fleet commanded by the famous Jean Bart. When he was recalled, his successor allowed the Frenchmen to escape his vigilance, and to begin a series of attacks on English and Dutch shipping. Piloted by a Jacobite exile named Thetford, they entered Druridge Bay, and sacked Widdrington, burning the houses and castle and doing damage to the value of £6,000. Though no compensation appears to have been offered by the government, collections were taken over the next couple of years in the churches of Northumberland and Durham with a view to reducing the villagers' sufferings.

A vast roundabout, looking very much out of place in such rural surroundings, heralds the recently reconstructed length of road that runs north to the red row of Chevington—now just known as Red Row—and to East Chevington and Broomhill nearby. These are just pit villages with few amenities; the shops, for instance, being concentrated in Red Row, where a number of modern houses relieve the monotony of the pit raas.

One wonders what the inhabitants of Acklington think of the various metamorphoses their village has undergone. When it was first founded by Eadlac's People, it was presumably as agricultural as any other, but as a member of the barony of Warkworth, it served for many years as a kind of handmaiden to the castle there; its smithy, for instance, working iron and shoeing the castle horses.

At a Muster of the Middle Marches in Elizabethan times the village could only furnish one horseman "able in horse and harness", but eleven footmen, seven of them armed with spears and defensive armour, three with spears only, and one with a petronell. By 1715 the place is described just as a large village with a colliery nearby, but in 1775 a foundry was built. No less an engineer than the great Smeaton was the creator of the dam in the River Coquet at Acklington Park which provided a fifteen-foot head of water to turn the wheels. Later the foundry became a 'woollen manufactory', now defunct, though the weir still remains as a reminder of the village's industrial past.

The next source of employment in Acklington was the provision of a mart alongside the main-line station half a mile west of the village, where great numbers of cattle and sheep are still sold. The real revolution came, however, with the building of an airfield nearby, from which, once its warlike commitments had ended, helicopters achieved a great reputation for their rescue work, especially over the sea. The modern houses that were built for the married quarters provided what was probably a welcome addition to the hitherto sleepy old stone-built village, though they have done nothing to add to its appearance. Since then the wheel of events has turned once again, and in a less welcome direction, for signposts provide a grim reminder that the airfield has now been turned into an open prison.

Coquetdale

WHEN Dippie Dixon wrote that lovely book *Upper Coquetdale*, which still remains the guide, companion and friend of anyone writing about this part of Northumberland, he defined the area with which he was concerned as that part of the dale from its inception as far as Brinkburn—that is to say to the Newcastle-to-Coldstream road. For the purposes of this chapter, with its rather different title, I propose to descend as far as Felton on the Great North Road, and to have a look at the same time at the neighbouring valley of the Aln, better known as Whittingham Vale. Between them, the two dales provide both some of the finest scenery and the longest historical associations to be found in the county, for the whole area is dotted not only with ancient churches and Border towers, but distinguished by what remains of two Roman roads, and by trackways and camps that take one back into pre-history. It is a strip of Northumberland that, beginning on the Scottish Border, includes the southern parts of the Cheviots and the wild country associated with them; then gradually widens out into a more fertile countryside interrupted only by the moors to the north of Rothbury.

The Coquet, one of the finest salmon rivers in all England, has been the subject of endless fishing songs; indeed almost a subject of veneration to those who enjoy the sport. So full of fish was it once that "it was nowse* then but to fling in an' pull oot by tweeses and threeses, if ye had sae mony heuck on", while trout were so thick at the Thrum (the narrows below Rothbury) "that if

* Nowt, nothing.

ye had stricken the end o' year gad into the watter amang them it
wad amaist hae studden upreet". So,

> The Coquet for ever, the Coquet for aye!
> The Coquet the King o' the stream an' the brae;
> From his high mountain throne to his bed in the sea,
> Oh! where shall we find such a river as he?
> Then blessings be on him, and lang may he glide,
> The fisherman's home and the fisherman's pride.

One of the best ways to approach Coquetdale is from Elsdon
over Billsmoor to Hepple. Here the river has forsaken its first fine
careless rapture in its descent from the hills, and is lazily threading its way along the haughs below Simonside. Once an important
place and the centre of a barony, Hepple now consists of a few
houses straggling along the road, with the foot-hills of the Cheviots
on one side, the river on the other. At the west end lie a couple
of farm steadings and, further west still, the site of the medieval
village. The most striking feature is the remains of a Border tower
half hidden by trees, once the schoolmaster's house and now, I
am delighted to say, undergoing extensive repair. It is in the list
of 1415 that it first appears in history, when it is mentioned as
one of the six towers belonging to Robert Ogle; but it seems prob-
able that it was built nearly a hundred years earlier. In the Border
Survey of 1541, however, "at Hephell ys a town of thinherytance
of the lorde Ogle decayed in the roofes and scarcely in good re-
pac'ons", a remark which is of double significance. Not only does
it reflect the risks run by anyone living so near the Border at
the hands of the marauding bands of reivers from Scotland (and
incidentally from neighbouring Redesdale as well), but it provides
a clue to the derivation of the village's name which, believe it or
not, is connected with dog-roses, for this is the *halh*, or Haugh,
where Hips (the fruit of the rose) were to be found. Originally,
the tower would have been some forty to fifty feet high, and it is
known that the barrel-vaulting of the basement, into which the
most valuable of the horses and the milking cows would be driven
when an attack appeared imminent, was seventeen feet high. Repeated efforts have been made to use the tower, as in so many
other cases, as a kind of quarry from which to take building stone.
So hard, however, was the mortar with which the huge stones
are bonded that they have often been in vain.

A little further up the dale, one crosses a tiny burn and encounters a sign bearing the words "Military Vehicles 15 mph"; for this is Holystone, where the valley road is joined by the Roman road from High Rochester that winds its way across the moors now used as an Artillery Range. Where once Paulinus baptized the Northumbrians and later a cell of Benedictine nuns prayed for their souls, there rumble the Land Rovers and lorries, and even the guns, of the soldiery who come here for firing practice. The Roman road, now partly lost, partly re-metalled for the use of the military, once joined Dere Street to its offshoot the Devil's Causeway, thus completing a triangle whose apex is some five miles north of Corbridge.

Three hundred yards behind the Salmon Inn lies the chief glory of Holystone, for here there bubbles forth a spring of water once known as St Ninian's, but now as the Ladies', Well. It was in this spring that at Easter 627 Paulinus is reputed to have baptized no less than three thousand (presumably not all at one sitting) and it is the stone commemorating that event that gave the village its name. Surrounded by tall beeches and rhododendrons, it now supplies a shadowy pool to which a rim of masonry has been added in the eighteenth century; a reminder, even to the least imaginative, of a time when Northumbria was a cradle of English Christianity.

The Ladies after whom the spring was named were, of course, the inhabitants of Holystone Priory, which by 1291 housed twenty-seven nuns, four lay brothers, three chaplains and a master. They suffered grievously from the depredations of the Scots. Of the priory itself nothing remains but the name of the farm which, in its walled farmyard, with the curious dovecots at the corners, forms such an important part of the village. There is another spring, just west of the tiny church, which now feeds a 'pant' or drinking fountain. It is a characteristic of so many of our 'saintly' wells that they are to be found near Roman roads which, for hundreds of years, gave the only easy access to the countryside. This one is the well of St Mungo, the Scottish saint originally named Kentigern, whom we have already met at Simonburn.

Appropriately enough in a village where the houses have just been plumped down where fancy dictated, there have been recorded throughout the years a number of eccentrics. One of them was Ned Allan, the weaver, brother of the notorious Jamie Allan, piper to the Duke of Northumberland. In the latter days of the eighteenth century, Ned attained a tremendous reputation for his skill in spearing eels. Indeed he found fishing, and the hunting of otters with his dog Tug-em, preferable to any kind of work, and when asked to help a neighbouring farmer with his harvest, replied firmly "Ye should sow ne mair nor ye can shear. A'll help nane o' ye."

When Ned died, the local schoolmaster was moved to compose an epitaph that finished up:

> The amphibious otter, now secure
> On Coquet's peaceful shore,
> May roam at large, for Ned and Tug
> Will never harm him more.
> Up Swindon burn he may return,
> When salmon time comes on;
> For poor old Ned in his cold bed
> Sleeps sound at Holystone.

Above the sharp bend in the Coquet known as the Devil's Elbow and lying alongside, if not on the top of, the river's original course, is Harbottle.* From time immemorial this has been one of the most important military outposts in the country. Its name has been translated by generations of historians as the Buildings of the Host—in other words, barracks. But this is surely hindsight? Even if the place did not previously house a garrison, however, it certainly did so from the days of the Normans onwards, for in 1160 a castle was built here by the united efforts of Henry II and the Bishop of Durham, which for centuries was to house the principal garrison of the Middle March. As one might imagine, it had a stormy history, being sacked by the Scots, rebuilt more strongly and besieged again, this time without success. In 1515, as the official residence of the Keeper of Redesdale, it received Margaret Tudor, sister of Henry VIII, widow of James IV of Scotland and now Countess of Angus. Here she gave birth to a daughter— another Margaret—whose grandson was to become James I of England. In the seventeenth century, when the castle finally fell into ruin, the stones were used for the new Harbottle Castle which

* The Dwelling of the Hireling(s).

stands to the east of the village. Two rows of solidly built stone houses, a United Reformed church and manse, and a pub, complete the village, to which a rather unpleasant-looking Gothic fountain adds very little.

The last village (if you can honestly call it a village) up the dale is the Homestead by the Alwin (a tributary of the Coquet), in other words Alwinton—pronounced Allenton. By now the valley has narrowed to a mere cleft in the Cheviots. But this is a strategic, and therefore an historic, part of the county, for on the higher ground above the little Alwin, as it rushes down past Kidland Lee to join the Coquet, there winds that prehistoric track known as Clennell Street. This is one of several which make their way over the Cheviot ridges into Scotland, for here we are less than eight miles from the Border: that is, as the crow flies, though it must be admitted that he would have to fly pretty high.

In the course of its history Clennell Street has seen the passing of the iron-age men who built the camps that dot the Coquet valley, the early explorations of the Angles and Scandinavians who succeeded them, the passing of the monks of Newminster on their way to their sheep runs at Kidland, and the reivers running their stealthy forays. Up Clennell Street, on Days of Truce, rode the Wardens of the Middle Marches, in order to meet their opposite numbers on the heights of Windygyle. It was at just such a Day of Truce that Lord Russell met his death—an event commemorated to this day by a cairn of stones that bears his name, though it probably dates from prehistoric times. Then it was the smugglers creeping along with their panniers full of salt or whisky that trod Clennell Street, until at last it has reverted to the use that has never altered since long before the Monks of Newminster—the passage of the shepherds and their sheep.

As a meeting of the ways, and a centre for the scattered population of the Cheviots, Alwinton has always enjoyed an importance out of all proportion to its size. Nowadays it consits of a farm, an old-fashioned pub (the 'Rose and Thistle') a post office and a few low stone houses scattered in the shape of an L along one side of a green bisected by the tiny Hosedon Burn. Hardly a trace of the old village with its primitive dwellings is now to be found.

It is the Shepherds' Show for which Alwinton is famous. Other agricultural shows come and go, but this one, still very much confined to sheep and shepherds and the rural skills, seems to go on for ever. Once a year Alwinton really comes to life to the sound of the Northumbrian pipes, the grunting of the wrestlers and the baaing of sheep. Both shepherds and their dogs can compete for prizes, the wives show off their home cooking, and the stick carvers the products of their art, while the trail-hounds race over the fells.

For the remainder of the year it is the grand old church of St Michael that provides the principal attraction. Built on the hillside, it is one of the most interesting in the county. By the churchyard gate stands a little low building with a roof of stone slabs, fastened in the traditional manner with sheep's shank-bones. Incredibly, it is reputed once to have been the vicarage. It is difficult, however, to imagine any rector, vicar, minister or curate—for all four titles have been applied to the incumbent at different times —so small and so poverty-stricken that he would have put up with such a dwelling. For years it was used, as at Chollerton, as a 'parish stable' for the use of parishioners riding to church from a distance, and to house the bier at funerals.

Having once passed through the gate, it comes as something of a surprise to find oneself treading a path consisting entirely of tombstones, while the floor of the church itself gives much the same impression. More remarkable still is the effect created by building the church on land that slopes up towards the east. In the first place it results in a west end of formidable height while, in the second, it means that no less than ten steps lead up from the nave to the chancel, as well as a further three to the altar.

East of Alwinton, and therefore among less austere surroundings, lies the Lower Town, that is to say Netherton, a little village of no particular distinction, to be followed by another even smaller, originally christened—because of its position on an exposed ridge —the Windswept or Snowy place: in other words Snitter. In the March Laws, which laid down the details of the watches to be kept against the marauding Scots, it was at the "Water of Wreigh" nearby that "Four men in the watch of the inhabitants of Snitter" were expected to do their duty.

Inevitably, Thropton was once a much more important place than it is now, due mainly to the fact that it was founded at what was then a Crossroads, which incidentally gave the village its name. In sparsely populated districts even the smallest hamlet usually boasts either a church or chapel, but in this respect Thropton might seem to be overdoing it a bit. On the descent from Snitter one passes first the tiny C. of E. church of St Andrew: then, in the middle of the village, the delightful little Catholic Church of All Saints. For nearly three hundred years Thropton has been the centre of Catholicism in the valley and it was towards the end of the seventeenth century that the Reverend Roger Mitford left in his will money "to make provision for the support of a priest to minister to the Catholics in and around Rothbury." The present church was completed in 1811 when Thropton Hall, to which the earlier chapel was attached, was pulled down. There must also have been some kind of almshouse in the village, for attached to the west end of All Saints' church is an old plaque which reads

Founded for ancient poor widows within the parish of Rothbury by Dame Mary Charleton of Hesleyside, eldest daughter and co-heir of Sir Edward Widdrington of Cartington Bart both in this county. She dyed 8 April 1703 *aetat suae* 71. *Requiescat in pace*.

Only a little further along the street, and on the same side, stands the United Reformed Church with its sprightly bell-cot, while near the west end of the village is to be found the Meeting House of the Plymouth Brethren.

Despite what seems almost a surfeit of religious opportunity, Thropton has not only had its fair share of eccentrics but, within living memory, one at least who cared little for the virtues of sobriety. This was Joe the Nip, so called because, once he had retired, he proceeded to invest his pension in continuous nips of rum. At the age of ninety, he was persuaded to enter an Old People's Home, but it was not long before he had escaped and, turning up once more at 'The Three Wheaten Heads', demanded his usual nip, complaining that he could no longer stand the inhabitants of the home, who were "aal either aad or deif".

Through the village runs that same Wreigh Burn (pronounced 'rithe') that we have encountered at Snitter, and whose name is derived from the Old English *wearg*, a felon; for this is probably where malefactors were drowned, as an alternative to hanging. Of the medieval hospital that once stood on its banks nothing remains except for a slab of stone, now in the grounds of Wreigh-

I

burn House, that bears on it the cross of the Knights Hospitaller of St John of Jerusalem.

Last but not least among the sights of Thropton is the tower, built probably in the fourteenth century, which figures in the Border Survey of 1541 as "a little tower of thinherytaunce of Sr Cuthbt Ratclyffe, Knight". When, in the Fifteen, the Jacobites of Northumberland under James Radcliffe, Earl of Derwentwater, marched through here on their way to Rothbury, it was already in disrepair. Since then it has been completely restored and modernized. As it is really a bastle; in other words, lower, simpler and more rectangular than a tower, it is easy from the street to mistake it for a house of no particular distinction.

It is rather sad to find that Alnham (known or pronounced at various times as Anham, Yeldom and even Yarwell), though it was once, like Alwinton, an important place in the commercial life of the Border and able to muster twenty-two men "able in horse and harness", has since dwindled almost to nothing. Exposed as it was to Scottish raids, despite the presence of the garrison at Harbottle, the village must for centuries have led a precarious existence. The Earl of Northumberland, for instance, once made an impassioned protest to Henry VIII to the effect that the Scots had "brunte a town of mine called Alnham, with all the corne, hay and house-holde stuf in the said town"; then, rather as an after-thought, "also a woman". Perhaps it is inevitable that with the general depopulation of the countryside there now remain only Alnham House, the church and vicarage, a farm, and a school some little way from the village. Gone also are the old cockfighting days that included one contest in particular between Alnham and Nether-ton that was afterwards immortalized in verse. The Netherton birds, for some reason, were named after Napoleon's generals, those of Alnham after the English. In the semi-final Napoleon beat Wolfe,* but Wellington beat Ney, so

> Jim bagg'd Napoleon, and off he went;
> To Netherton cockin' the lad was bent;
> But Wellington lick'd him to his heart's content
> That verra day.

The church remains partly Norman, though much restored;

---

* There seems to have been some confusion here!

while the vicarage—now used as a youth hostel—is in the form of a vicar's peel or, to put it more correctly, a vicar's tower. Past the tower and the British fort, known as Castle Hill, runs the Salter's Road. Part of a prehistoric network of trackways, since used by pedlars, drovers, shepherds and smugglers, it joins Clennell Street on the Border line near Rory's Still, named after the gentleman of that name who used to distil the whisky that found its way into many a Border glass.

At Alnham we have reached the upper waters of the River Aln and the fertile valley that is more usually known as Whittingham Vale. Whittingham itself (pronounced, of course, Whittinjum) has been an important place ever since Hwita's People settled there in the early days of the Anglian colonization. In choosing a site near the spot where the Devil's Causeway is joined by the Holystone road, they were making use of the only decent roads in the county—those built by the Romans. And it is communications that have dictated the village's destiny ever since, the diversion of the old coach road from Newcastle to Coldstream and Edinburgh eventually leaving the place high and dry.

What Whittingham has lost in importance, however, it has gained in its air of almost unspoilt seclusion. One's first impression is of nice old stone houses and a profusion of trees, but there is more to Whittingham than that—much more. Entering the village from the Coldstream road, one passes a pant, or drinking fountain, apparently surmounted by a shepherd and his dog, but actually by the third Lord Ravensworth of Eslington Hall, to whose memory it was erected. Nearby stands the Castle Inn, where the Wellington coach used to draw up on its way to Edinburgh, while on the other side of the little stone bridge there nestle a number of creeper-clad houses with red-tiled roofs, known as the Church Town.

There is a fine vicarage, built in the reign of William IV, which is not so vast as it looks, having been reduced in size without its proportions being visibly affected. Whittingham, as one of the most important places in Northumbria, has always held an important place in Church affairs. In A.D. 737 it belonged to King Ceolwulf, and it was in his day, it is thought, that the church of St Bartholomew—which still retains its original Saxon tower—was first built. It seems fairly certain also that Whittingham, with its two fords over the River Aln, was the Twyford where, according to Bede, a great synod assembled in the year 664 and chose Cuthbert to be Bishop of Lindisfarne.* Given such an historic church it now seems almost incredible that anyone could have been such a vandal as the Reverend William Goodenough, or so unfeeling as his architect John Green, when they lopped the top off the beautiful Saxon tower and replaced it with the present Victorian excrescence. Perhaps we should be thankful that they did not turn their attention to the inside, where plenty of thirteenth-century work remains in evidence, including some handsome tracery in a window in the lady chapel that gives on to the vestry.

The fact that Whittingham boasts not one but two squires is made clear by the marking of the two front pews on each side of the aisle with the letter 'C' for Callaly Castle and 'E' for Eslington Hall respectively. At the back of the church is a pew marked 'V' to show that it is reserved for the vicarage servants.

So much for the Church Town. There remains the southern part of the village, which is just as interesting in its way. Here is to be found a kind of wooded green, where stands, rather surprisingly, a nineteenth-century court house replete with gables and mullioned windows, which is still in use. Almost next door to it is the peel tower, in 1416 the property of William Heron, of a famous Northumbrian family who reigned also at Chipchase and at Ford. The basement has the usual tunnel vaulting and the walls are nine feet thick, but the tower itself has been a good deal altered, to allow of its being used as an almshouse for four old ladies.

And what a past Whittingham has had; not only ecclesiastical but military. At first it was, of course, the Scots, whose frequent incursions into Northumberland included that of 1314 when the tower was formally besieged, though without success. Later on, and right up to Stuart times, it was still the Scots, but on a less official basis. Sir Cuthbert Collingwood, the deputy Warden of the Middle March, for instance, barely escaped with his life on one occasion when the reivers of Teviotdale attacked him at Eslington.

Next came the Civil War, when there appeared one day four hundred Roundheads, singing psalms and demanding breakfast; while in 1648 Cromwell's horse entered the place once more, this

---

* The other possibility is Alnmouth.

time capturing Lieutenant Colonel Millet and two hundred of his men. In the Fifteen the inhabitants followed George Collingwood in support of the Old Pretender, only to see him executed for his pains, and the estate of Eslington sequestrated. In the words of "Lord Derwentwater's Farewell",

> And fare thee well, George Collingwood,
> Since fate has put us down;
> If thou and I have lost our lives
> Our king has lost his crown.

A hundred years later, when it was ordained that the militia should be enlisted by ballot instead of being provided by the landlords, there were riots not only in Hexham, where the yeomanry fired on the mob, but at Morpeth as well, whence the rioters descended on Whittingham and burnt the militia rolls.

But it is Whittingham Fair for which the village was best known. Held on 24th September each year, it used to attract the country folk from far and wide. It is said that on one occasion a gang of Irishmen who had come to be hired for the harvest went berserk with drink, 'took' the fair and smashed everything within sight, and that the village joiner, seizing a fencing rail, mowed them down in swathes and, single-handed, beat them off. This also was the inspiration of that lovely song which Whittingham, along with other villages, claims as its own, and which begins:

> Are you going to Whittingham Fair?
> Parsley, sage, rosemary and thyme;
> Remember me to one who lives there
> For once she was a true love of mine.

Anyone who, like myself, is moved by the Northumbrian virtues of ruggedness and massive simplicity should visit the village of Eadwulf's people—in other words Edlingham. Here they will see, in addition to a pleasant little estate village, the grand old church of St John, which looks as if it has never altered during the eight or nine hundred years of its existence. At first sight it gives the impression of an empty shell, for the original roof has been replaced by one that is almost flat, so that at close quarters it is virtually invisible. There is a lovely Norman arch and, curious to relate what looks like another *outside* the east window, though this is presumably a Victorian addition. The crowning glory of the place, however, is the tower with its pyramidical roof, its enormously thick walls, its 'shott'* windows that are virtually arrow-slits, and the holes in the doorway connecting the tower to the church, that are designed to hold a locking bar. All in all, there seems little doubt that it was originally built to serve two purposes, first as a kind of peel tower where the villagers could take refuge in case of attack and secondly as a prison in which they could bar up anyone they captured.

On a knowe in the field behind the church stands all that remains of Edlingham Castle, knee-deep in the muck of the cattle that use it for shelter. There are no longer any signs of a gate house, or of 'mansions' within the barmkin or courtyard, but there still survive the ruins of a barmkin wall.

The latter part of the seventeenth century saw a series of witch-hunts without parallel before or since, and it was not many years after the junketings at Riding Mill that a poor old woman of Edlingham named Margaret Stothard was brought before Henry Ogle Esq. Once suspicion had been aroused there was no end to the stories of her activities which were forthcoming. She had bewitched a calf, which "went perfectly mad", had prevented cheese from forming, had caused the death of someone's baby, and so forth. John Miles, the agent at the Castle, who ought to have known better, deposed that, lying awake one Sunday night, he "did heare a great blast of wind, as he thought, goe by his window, and immediately following there was something fell with a great weight upon his heart and gave a great crye like a catt, and then after another in the same manner, and just as those were ended there appeared a light at his bedd foot and did in the same light see Margaret Stothard, or her vission, to the best of his knowledge".

Happily Henry Ogle remained unimpressed, and Margaret went free.

In Northumberland, as in other counties, there exist a number of homesteads spawned in Norman and medieval times and known therefore as the New Town—Newton near Corbridge, Newton Park, Newton Underwood and Newton-by-the-Sea among others. Lying, like Edlingham, between the Aln and the Coquet, and, as

---

* Splayed.

its name implies, on the higher ground to the west of the A1, is another of them in the shape of Newton-on-the-Moor. It is not so long ago that the Great North Road virtually passed through the village, but its replacement north of Felton by a dual carriageway on a slightly different line has left the place high and dry, turning it into a delightful back-water. Time, however, had already caused changes in the village itself. Newton Hall, built in 1772, but since altered and added to by the great John Dobson, still survives in its wooded park. So does the attractive little pant erected in 1914 by the tenants of the estate to commemorate the golden wedding of Fitzherbert and Cecilia Widdrington. The chapel, however, which still bears the inscription "Methodist New Connexion 1852" has been turned, first into a school and since into a dwelling house, a fate that has also overtaken the school that succeeded it.

This is a village largely made up of single-storey houses with pleasant red pantile roofs, that was once a good deal bigger than it is now, when the inhabitants worked in the neighbouring pit and in the quarries near Longframlington. In those days there were no less than three pubs, of which only one survives, with the curious title of 'The Cook and Barker Arms'. This started life as the 'Moorcock', but owes its present name to the marriage in 1757 of the sister of the Reverend Dr Barker, Master of Christ's College, Cambridge to Samuel Cook of Newton Hall, and the subsequent quartering of their arms. It was their grandson who succeeded to the Widdrington Estates and changed his name accordingly.

On the same side of the village street is a blank wall of no particular interest to the uninitiated, but actually forming part of a seventeenth-century manor house with a delightful frontal aspect which, unfortunately, few are privileged to see. Opposite stands a long, mainly single-storey, building—the Jubilee Hall—in which church services are conducted (hence the belfry), but the other end of which has been converted into a dwelling house.

Past the present Hall a road runs southwards in the direction of that monument to misguided generosity, the Swarland Estate. It was at the time of the Great Depression, when thousands of shipyard workers on the Tyne were out of work, that a wealthy Yorkshireman conceived the idea of settling them on one-and-a-half acre plots, on which they could presumably grow enough to feed themselves and have a little left over. The scheme never really worked, yet the present inhabitants have retained, or developed, a feeling of community—and an association to prove it—that almost, if not quite, entitles the place to be called a village.

A little further and you reach the main road to Coldstream at Longframlington, the homestead where the people of Framela— that is to say, Little Fram—once lived. Like so many main-road villages, the best is never seen as we rush from A to B and back again, for the bulk of it lies to the west. Only three pubs are left out of the six that once graced the village. It comes as something of a surprise to find that one of them is named 'The Granby', the explanation being that descendants of the Manners family of Etal once owned much of the village, and the inn was called after their distinguished relation, the Marquess of Granby. The inhabitants of Longframlington are an independent lot, a state of mind which they attribute to the absence in later years of a squire, which has resulted in many of them becoming owner-occupiers of land allotted to them on the enclosure of the Common. Outsiders used to reckon that they took this business of independence a little too far, for "the folk of Framlington say that none but whores and blackguards marry: honest folk take each other's word". Yet the village is well served from a religious point of view. St Mary's is a delightful church, dating back to Norman times and with that rarity in the county, a medieval porch. Moreover the place boasts one of the oldest Presbyterian congregations in England. One of the Hazleriggs—perhaps the father of Sir Arthur, who became such a stalwart of the Parliamentary party in the Civil War— maintained a Presbyterian Minister in his own house; after which the congregation met in another private house until 1739, when the present United Reformed church, with its agreeable belfry, was built.

At the northern end of Longframlington, and shielded by some gloomy-looking trees, is Embleton Hall, whose oldest wing dates back to 1675 or thereabouts. Equally interesting is Rookwood House in the western part of the village, opposite the Green, with its charming little walled garden. The date is 1717 and the initials W.T.M. over the door relate perhaps to one of the Manners. The Green itself is reputed to mask the remains of a Roman marching camp, for Villa Lane follows the original line of the Devil's Causeway.

No less than seventy-six council houses have been built over the last few years, and the villagers will tell you with pride that as a result there are no longer any young couples 'living in'. Unfortunately an estate of 'executive houses' (dreadful word!) is contemplated, and Longframlington is unlikely ever to be the same again.

If, for the purposes of this book, we are to insist on the Great North Road as the eastern limit of Coquetdale we must end our present journey at Felton, a village that actually bestrides the A1, though that part of it that lies to the south of the Coquet is, strictly speaking, Thirston. The two are connected by a splendid medieval bridge, now supplemented by a modern one better suited to the motor age.

Rather surprisingly for a river village, the place was originally christened the Homestead in Open Country (which is the original meaning of 'field'). Since then it has seen a good deal of history in the making. It has been intimately—too intimately—involved in the incursion into Northumberland of Scottish armies, while later on its inhabitants were so outraged by King John's taxation methods that in 1216 they were ready to do homage to the Scottish king rather than put up with them any longer; only to have their village burnt to ashes as a punishment. In Tudor times it was the Scottish reivers who put the fear of God—or the Devil—into them, while in the Fifteen they welcomed the Northumbrian Jacobites, who were joined here by seventy gentlemen from the other side of the Border. They must have learnt their lesson, however, for thirty years later, when Butcher Cumberland passed through on his way to Culloden, they showed such enthusiasm that his royal highness was pleased to allude to the "loyal little village of Felton".

To anyone passing through the village along the A1, its most noteworthy aspect must be the awkward hill that leads into it from the south past the gloom of Thirston House; together with the rustic appearance of the houses on the hill that leads northwards. It is an impression that is unfortunately somewhat impaired by the council houses at the top, many of which are occupied by retired people. The opening of the Morpeth by-pass has brought Newcastle within less than an hour's run by car, and has not only resulted already in a number of the older houses being altered to suit commuters, but has created the threat, as at Longframlington, of a commuter estate.

Like Longframlington, Felton hides its light under a bushel, for the best of the village lies not along the main road at all, but on a hill above the Coquet, a little distance to the west. Indeed a stranger could be excused for not knowing it existed, for to get there you must leave Felton proper by means of the Swarland road, and then fork left.

Here, in its extensive grounds, stands Felton Park, the home for so long not only of that great Catholic family the Riddells, but, for a few years of the nineteenth century, of their famous race-horse Dr Syntax. It is the church of St Michael, however, that really catches the eye. At first sight, the existence of an almost flat roof where once there was a steeply pitched one, gives it an impression, as at St John's Edlingham, of being without a roof altogether; which once it almost was, for certain gentlemen unspecified made away with a great quantity of the lead with which it is covered.

To my way of thinking this is the most impressive church in Northumberland, with one of those strange, primitive belfries, perched on a buttress like a chimney breast, which still houses a pre-Reformation bell. Much of the church, and it is a pretty large one, is of the thirteenth and fourteenth centuries; wide, squat, and massive beyond belief. At the east end of one of the aisles is a window, the whole of whose top part (some six feet high and six feet across) is carved out of a single stone. Best of all is the ponderous porch, with its extraordinary slab roof, once described as resembling a great stone cave.

In the stirring days of the sixteenth century, if there was one family that delighted more than another in harrying the Church, it was the Lisles of Felton. For years successive knights and their progeny carried on a running battle with the canons of nearby Brinkburn Priory. It was in 1514 that the sorely tried prior complained that a number of the brethren had been put in the stocks by Sir Humphrey Lisle's men, whose master had expelled the Vicar of Felton (who was also a canon of Brinkburn) from his living and substituted a secular parson. The unfortunate vicar did not dare, for fear of the Lisles, to do anything about the matter, other than weep on the prior's shoulder, and his timidity may well have inspired the rhyme that has been sung in nurseries all over England.

> The little priest of Felton,
> The little priest of Felton,
> He killed a mouse within his house,
> And nobody there to help him.

II

Glendale and its Neighbours

IN the days when the road to Edinburgh by way of Wooler and Coldstream was used as much as, if not more than, the Great North Road, the villages that grew with it not unnaturally gained an importance which, with the exception of Wooler itself, they have not enjoyed since. Nevertheless, as in the case of Whittingham, what they have lost in commercial importance they have gained in atmosphere, and it is no bad thing that instead of rushing through them regardless one is now able to pause and, as someone once put it, smell the flowers. Flowers, incidentally, that are all the sweeter for being grown almost in the shadow of the Cheviots.

One such village is Glanton—the Homestead by the Lookout Hill (in other words Glanton Pike). Once nearly as large as Whittingham, it is still a fair-sized village by Northumbrian standards, and it was to the Mile Farm that James IV sent his herald, Islay, to parley with the Earl of Surrey before Flodden. It was at Glanton also that 180 Royalists (fast asleep, as usual) were captured by Colonel Sanderson almost without a struggle.

During the period between 1763, when this section of the Coldstream road was completed, and the twentieth century, when the village was by-passed, Glanton grew into a commercial centre of considerable significance, distributing the goods that came by carrier from Newcastle to a district where both quarrying and agriculture were booming. In a countryside so sparsely populated no one seems to have been prepared to endow a church, leaving a vacuum that the Presbyterians were glad to fill, following it up soon after with a tiny school which now serves as a garage for the manse.

With the advent of the railways the importance of Glanton diminished, and the finishing touch was given by the diversion of the main road. The saddler, the baker and the brewhouse have disappeared, and the 'Old Post House' has taken the place, not of a coaching inn, as one might expect, but of the original post office. The 'Turk's Head', moreover was renamed the 'Queen's Head' in order to celebrate Queen Victoria's Jubilee, though the 'Red Lion' continues under its original name. Even the famous Kippin (or Kippie) Well has moved, or rather its accessories have. Its name derives from the fact that the water of the spring had to be caught or 'kepped' in pails or jugs and, as can be imagined, it was a splendid place for gossip, as well as a source of healing for sickly children whose fate it was to be wrapped in blankets and placed under the spout. Thanks to an enlightened County Council, the original stone trough, complete with the inscription that commemorates the piping of the water into the village, has been united to a sundial from one of the old cottages and placed by the roadside at the north-east corner of the village.

Yet despite all these changes Glanton retains a certain charm that is due as much as anything to the width of the streets, that are lined incidentally with houses so intermingled that the inhabitants have had trouble from time to time in making out which rooms belong to which.

North of Glanton, and on the main road once more, lies Powburn, a straggling hamlet that is notable mainly for an inn which still displays the timetable for the Edinburgh coaches, and for the geological absurdity of Crawley Dene which cuts through the high ground separating the two valleys to the east of Glanton, thus connecting them together.

A glance at the map shows the extent to which this part of the county is dotted with the hill-forts and villages of our British ancestors. One of the most fertile areas for these remains is Bewick Moor, below which in the valley of the burn named after it, lies Eagwulf's Village—the modern Eglingham. Within living memory this was virtually an estate village, and it looks it. Pleasantly wooded, with neat gardens and hedges, the houses have now been sold off to the villagers. Weekenders, however, seem to be conspicuous by their absence, a state of affairs about which the inhabitants are rather pleased, for they have seen what has happened in other villages where a preponderance of second homes has been a very mixed blessing, their owners bringing their own groceries and etceteras, and causing trade to languish and with it the social life of the village.

As one approaches from the west, it is the Hall that first attracts attention. Once the home of a branch of that ancient Northumbrian family the Ogles, it still incorporates the remains of their sixteenth-century tower. Cromwell once stayed the night here (before it was rebuilt in 1704) and celebrated the occasion by having a flaming row with his host, Henry Ogle, before leaving.

Not far away stands St Maurice's church, much restored but still boasting a thirteenth-century tower which looks as if it has been used as a refuge in more stirring times. In the grounds stands a tiny two-storeyed building which one might be forgiven for thinking was a hearse-house, or a watch-place as at Dodding-ton.* Actually it was once the school, and if you care to search among the creepers you will find the date 1827 over the door.

Nearly opposite the 'Tankerville Arms'—once a rather primitive pub, but now raised to two floors—and next door to the charming little village shop and post office, stands a house of considerable age with, at its west end, a large pointed-arch window, or rather the tracery of such a window without either openings or glass. Now there is a story that a former vicar was once crossing to the Farne Islands—for the Vicar of Eglingham is also for some strange reason the Archdeacon of Lindisfarne—when he got into conversation with the boatman. "I knew Eglingham well by moonlight; you have a fine tithe-barn there, sir!" said the boatman. "Tithe-barn?" answered the vicar. "How do you know that?" "Many a time I have slept there," came the reply, "and left kegs of whisky. Why, sir, we always changed horses there!" Was this the tithe-barn in question then, or was the reference to the old barn at Cockhall, just three-quarters of a mile away on the Wooler road? Or is it true that the house once stored meal ground at the mill next door (where a fine village hall now stands) and that the 'window' was put there in the faint hope (for they were no re-specters of the church) of deceiving the Scottish reivers on their all too frequent visits?

So much for the country to the east of the Coldstream road.

* see page 145

To the west it is altogether different, varying from the little hopes and valleys that run down from the Cheviots to the rolling cornfields just south of Wooler. Here lie Branton, Ilderton and the two Middletons, looking like villages on the map, but on the ground just large farms or farming settlements, with a mass of fine buildings and perhaps a smithy and a pillar box. In addition Branton boasts a United Reformed church which, incredibly, has in its day accommodated congregations of up to five hundred.

Goodness knows how old Ingram is. All around, on the higher brackeny ground bordering the wide haughs of the Breamish that gave the place its name of the Meadow Village and now provide ideal picnicking places, are the remains of British settlements, culminating in the famous Greaves Ash, a prehistoric village covering no less than twenty acres. Once a much larger place than it is now, Ingram is reduced to two or three farmsteads, an Information Centre for the National Park, which covers all this part of the county; a house or two, a church and an enormous vicarage—all of them dotted about among the trees.

The principal feature of this village, which is really no longer a village, is a church as ancient as any, for parts of it date back to Edward the Confessor. Outside, the chief attraction is the low, squat tower so much in keeping with the spirit of the county, rebuilt with the original stones and still with the arrow-slits in the lower part. Ingram is only eight or nine miles from the Border as the crow flies, and in the days of the Border reivers suffered more than most. On one occasion they even managed to make off with the lead from the church roof. Nowadays it appears that the church is at risk once more, for a notice reads "Please shut this door and help us to keep the church free of bats".

North of Eglingham lies the higher ground of Bewick Moor and, nestling beneath it, the northernmost 'ingham', and the only one in Northumberland to be pronounced with a hard 'g'. This is Chillingham, with its magnificent castle and beautifully wooded park in which wild cattle have roamed ever since the park wall was built six hundred years ago but, apart from a few houses belonging to the Tankerville estate, no village worth the name.

Still further north lies Chatton—the 'tun' that Ceatta once founded. For such a small place it seems to have produced more than its share of interesting people. In the churchyard, for instance lie the remains—if they have not been washed away by the River Till in one of its more exuberant moods—of Joseph Dial, the mathematician and expert on navigation, whose 'jovial disposition and fondness for company led him into irregularities that clouded a vigorous genius". Pickled in booze, he survived to a ripe old age, but died in poverty.

Another connection with the navy is to be found in the ensign that hangs in Chatton church, which once adorned a French brig captured by Samuel Cook (the very same who inherited the Widdrington Estates),* who was born here. One of the village boys, James Service, was so inspired by this achievement (the capture of the Frenchman, not the inheritance of the estates) that he joined the navy forthwith. However he unfortunately lost a leg and, retiring from the sea, came back to his birthplace, where he divided his time between schoolmastering and writing some of the best poetry to come out of Northumberland. Impressionable as ever, he eventually emulated Joseph Dial, drank himself out of his job and finished up in the workhouse.

Historically speaking, Chatton once saw a good deal of life— or rather of death. Edward I spent some time here on his way to and from hammering the Scots, a favour which the latter returned with interest. The place also suffered grievously from the plague. In between whiles its inhabitants, like many others, spent a good deal of their time dodging the Scottish reivers, protected to some extent by two peel towers, one of which is now incorporated in the enormous vicarage. Since then nothing much seems to have happened, though in the early days of the eighteenth century Matthew Culley and his brother George (who had been the first pupil of the celebrated cattle breeder Robert Bakewell) lived at nearby Fowberry Tower and conducted the experiments in agriculture that made them world-famous.

It is a quiet, rather smug little village with a triangular green, a dull church with a steeply roofed tower, and a pleasant pub— the 'Percy Arms'. Some of the low stone cottages now house men working in forestry; others have been converted with remarkable foresight to accommodate retired agricultural workers.

* see page 135

The Cut at Seaton Sluice

Strother Farm, Holywell

Cambois: Staithes and power station

The cavernous porch of St Michael's, Felton

(*above*) The smithy at Hepscott

(*left*) Ten steps to the chancel: St Michael's, Alwinton

(*above right*) The court house and peel tower at Whittingham

(*below right*) Glanton Pike and the United Reformed church form a backcloth to the village

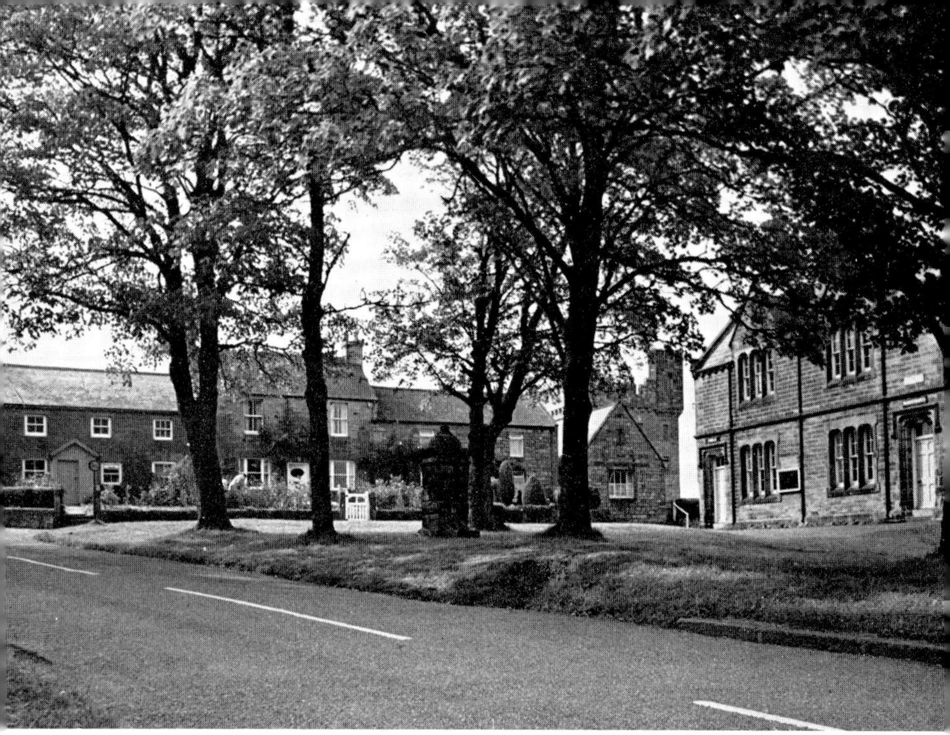

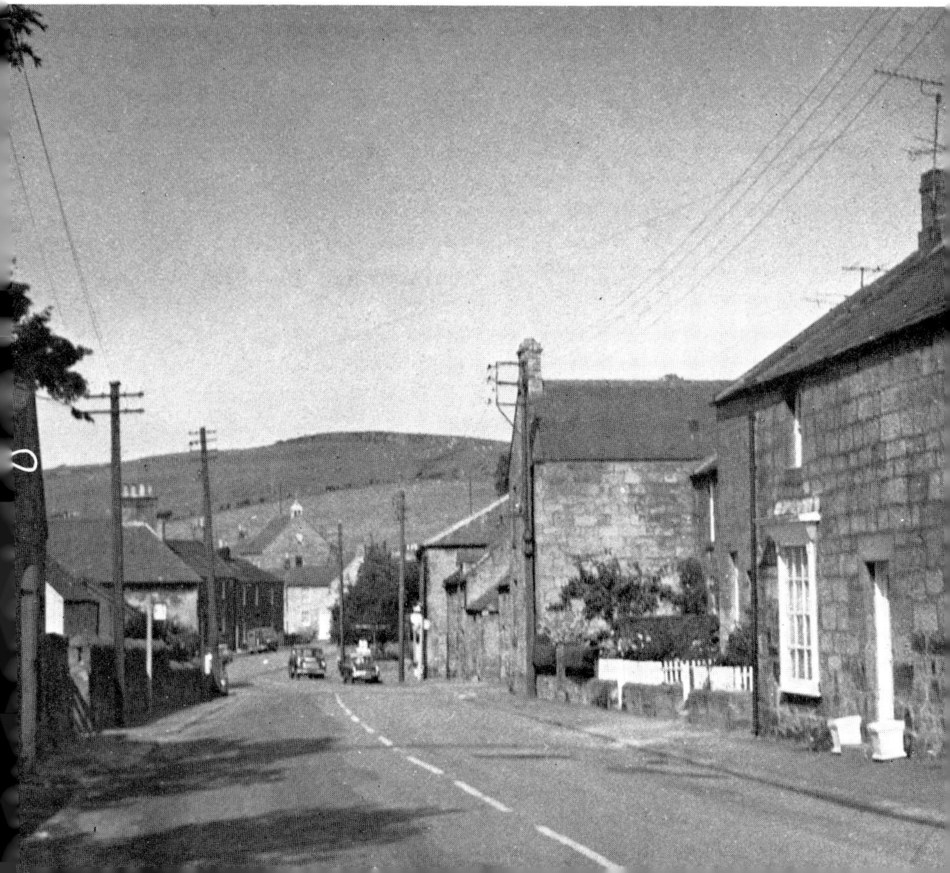

(*above*) The peel tower in Doddington

(*top right*) "We three Kings of Orient are": Kirknewton church
(*bottom right*) A fortified chancel: St Gregory's, Kirknewton

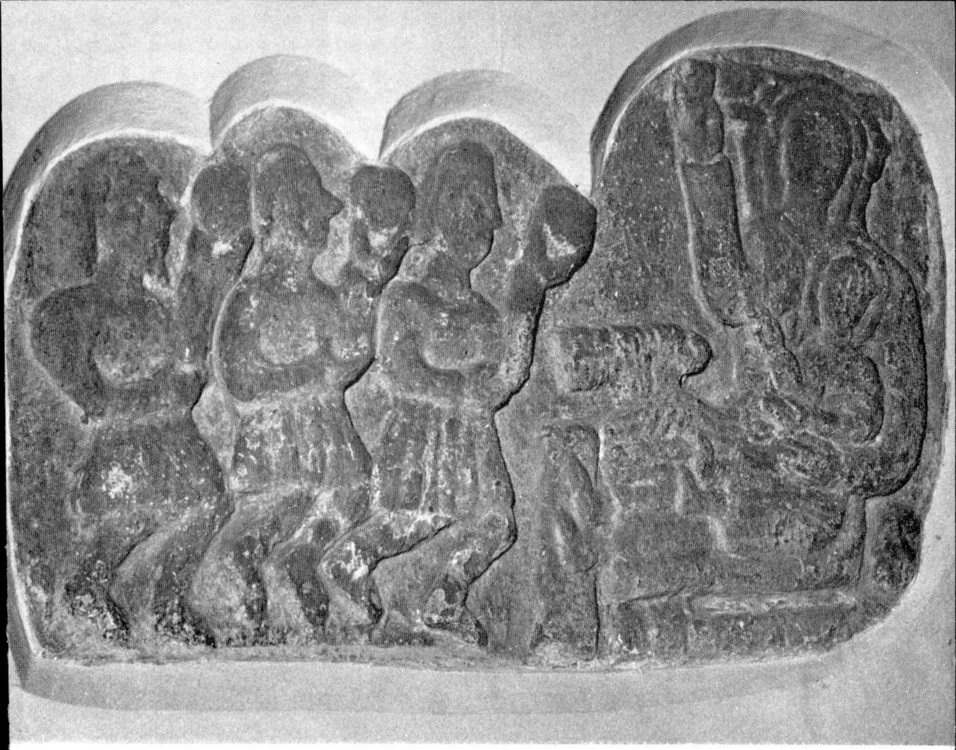

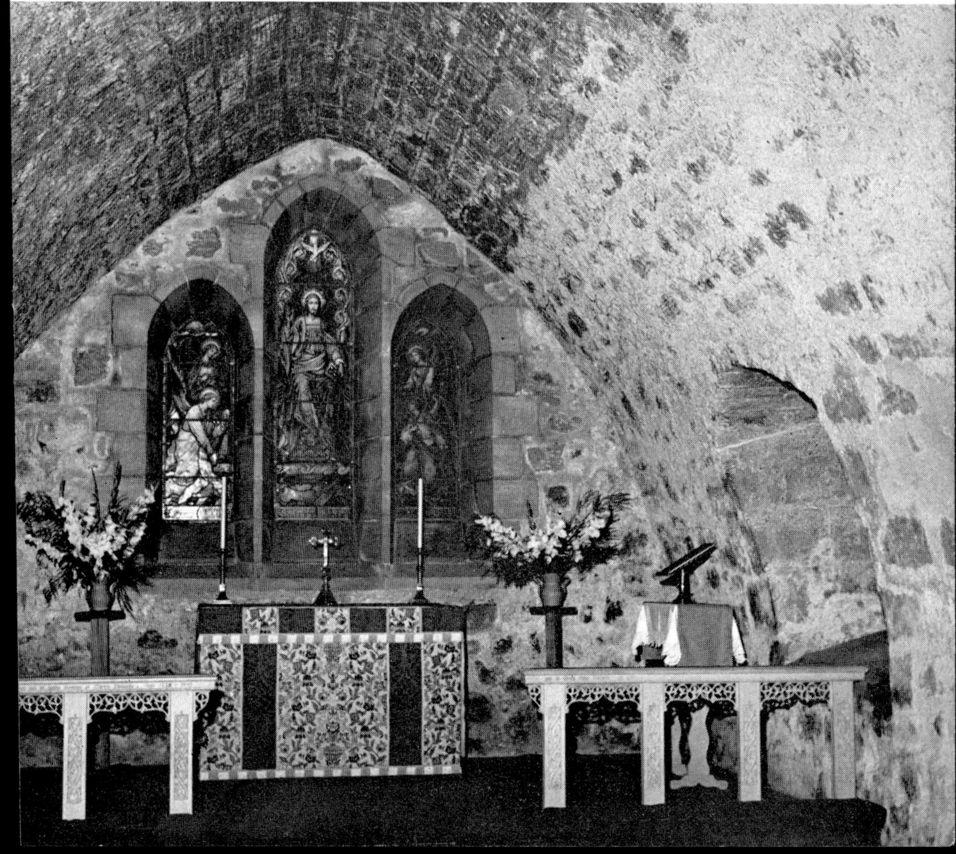

Ford: a model village

Branxton: the concrete menagerie

To the east of the Milfield plain (of which more in a moment) and huddled in a hollow among the trees, lies Doddington—the homestead of the people from Dod Law, just to the south of the village. ('Dod' or 'dodded' meaning rounded or polled, it is no accident that the polled black cattle known as Aberdeen Angus are always referred to in the Borders as 'Doddies'.) Nowadays the village consists mainly of two large farms, an odd, four-square vicarage, and a few houses dotted about the hollow. Once, however, this was a thriving community, known to its inhabitants for some obscure reason as Dorrington, and the subject of a popular tune for the Northumbrian pipes—"Dorrington lads yet". According to one of those jingles so common in the north of the county,

> It had four streets,
> Southgate and Sandgate and up the Cat Raw,
> The Tinklers' Street and Byegate Ha'.

The latter was an old farmhouse, and the Tinklers' Street was where the 'muggers'* set out their wares. Those were the days when the village housed weavers and shoemakers in addition to the farm hinds,† and was described in a survey of 1734 as "remarkable for its largeness, the badness of its houses and low situation, and perhaps for the greatest quantity of geese of any in its neighbourhood, and is distinguished from all the rest in the county except Branxton for having the chapel covered with heather and straw".

The church in question, dedicated to St Mary and St Michael, is doubly strange for, having been erected twenty degrees off the usual west-east line, there has since befallen it a worse fate still. Originally built in the thirteenth century with a chamber under the tower, the whole building was turned completely round in Victorian times, the chamber being converted into a chancel and the original chancel thrown into the nave, so that the church now faces west! In the corner of the churchyard stands one of those buildings which looks like a bier house, and which was actually erected in 1826—at a time when the 'resurrectionists' were active in their search for bodies to sell to the anatomy schools—as a

*Hawkers.
† Farm workers.

K

watch house. Hidden away in one of the farmyards stands all that remains of an L-shaped tower.

Right at the lowest point of the village, and marked by a fine cross, is the "Bonny Dod Well" which in Victorian times was described as "one of the largest and best springs in the country, which sends out a current sufficient to turn a mill". It would have to be a very small mill.

West of Doddington lies that topographical curiosity, the plain of Milfield, once a lake and still looking as if a period of rain would restore it to its original form. This is difficult country to farm, with soil that is thin and gravelly, and in the middle of it the Glen joins the Till. Both rivers have their origin in Cheviot country, one as Bowmont Water, the other as Breamish, and the speed with which water comes off the hills causes the Till to flood at the slightest provocation. Moreover it is full of deep holes, which makes bathing dangerous.

> Tweed said to Till
> "What makes ye run so still?"
> Till said to Tweed
> "Tho' ye run wi' speed,
> And I run slaw,
> Yet where ye drown ae man
> I drown twa."

When the kings of Bernicia vacated their palace at Yeavering, it was at Melmin, on the shores of what had been the lake, that they set up house. Indeed its very name Milfield commemorates some kind of Monument (perhaps a cross) that may well have been connected with the new palace. Much later—in fact just before Flodden—the village once again found a place in history when Lord Home, at the head of 3,000 horse from Scotland, was returning from an expedition in which he had burnt a number of villages. Ambushed by Sir William Bulmer amongst the tall broom of Milfield plain, he lost more than five hundred killed and four hundred prisoners, so that a raid which had started out so promisingly eventually became known by the Scots as the Ill Rode.

Considering its ancient importance, the present village comes as something of a disappointment, consisting, as it does, of a deserted airfield of World War Two, a council estate and a straggling line of houses largely concerned with agriculture, and very little else. Apart, that is to say, from one of the few saddlers now left in the county, who still makes a fair living catering for pony-club mounts rather than farm horses, and repairing pea-harvesters where once he stitched binder canvases.

Almost in the shadow of the Cheviots lies Kirknewton. In 1336 the place was known as the New Town in Glendale, and the addition of the word Church may well spring from the tradition that it was here that King Edwin married Ethelburga of Kent, in whose train came Paulinus. Near where Coupland Castle now stands, the latter is alleged to have spent thirty-six days instructing the converted and baptizing them in the River Glen.

Lying, as it does, just below the hill known as Yeavering Bell and not far from the site of King Edwin's palace, Kirknewton commands the valleys of College Burn and Bowmont Water, for it is here that they join to form the Glen. It is an unassuming little place with a farm in the centre and with gardens that are surrounded by high walls, giving the village a slightly Italianate look.

At first there seems to be nothing very much to attract one's attention. Even the church, extensively restored by John Dobson in the nineteenth century, seems to have little to offer. In fact it has a great deal. On entering the churchyard one notices at once the graves of the British and Commonwealth airmen who lost their lives when flying from the airfield at Milfield. In the opposite corner are those of four German airmen killed when their bomber crashed in the Cheviots in 1943. Once inside the innocent, even drab-looking, church one realizes that this is one of the strangest in the country—let alone in Northumberland. Elsewhere one comes across church towers built or altered to serve as fortresses, but here are a chancel and transept rebuilt from the Norman stone in the late thirteenth or early fourteenth centuries to serve as a refuge from the Scots. The chancel itself is very small and low, with all the appearance not of a church at all but the basement of a Border tower. With walls only three feet high, it consists entirely of a plain pointed vault into which the small windows penetrate. The south transept has no walls at all, being completely vaulted in the same way, and the two together epitomize the ruggedness, the durability and massiveness of the architecture that the Borderers found necessary to their survival.

Two remarkable carvings complete the curiosities of a church that it is worth travelling many miles to see. The first is a relief from the original Norman church, depicting the Adoration of the Magi; it shows the Madonna and Child by the manger, while the Wise Men, clad appropriately in kilts, offer their presents. The second consists of a fine grey tombstone with figures of a certain Andrew Bowrell and his wife, whose faces and hands have originally been of brass—a rarity in the North of England.

Not only is Kirknewton a very pleasant little place but presumably a healthy one as well, for during the eighteenth century two consecutive vicars between them served the church for no less than ninety-two years.

North of Kirknewton the Cheviots peter out into a series of rolling downs—unlikely country, one would think, in which to fight a battle if one could avoid it, for there are so many folds in the ground that it is hard to spot an enemy approaching. Yet it was under these conditions that James IV of Scotland chose to meet the Earl of Surrey, when he drew up his forces on Branxton Hill, preparatory to fighting the battle known to history as Flodden Field, an engagement that is commemorated by a monument near Branxton Stead.*

Branxton, like most of the villages near the Border, has seen more than its fair share of warfare since Brannoc—that is to say, Little Brand—set up his Homestead, and Flodden was only one of many occasions when English and Scots came to blows here. One Sunday a few years after the battle, for instance, five hundred Scots who had conducted a successful foray in the district, were ambushed by the young lord of Fowberry at the head of a hundred horse, and two hundred of them were taken prisoner.

It is ironic that in the midst of all this history there is virtually nothing old or exciting to be seen in Branxton itself, and it is not the famous battleground that visitors now come to see so much as Mr Fairnington's menagerie. Over goodness knows how many years, this member of a family of talented craftsmen has been modelling life-size animals in, of all things, concrete; and his garden of something over a quarter of an acre is now packed with more than a hundred brightly coloured animals that include a

* The King's Stone that stands just to the north of the Coldstream road has nothing to do with the battle, but marks the spot where the locals rendezvoused in time of invasion.

giraffe and a panda together with shrewdly observed groups of farm animals.

It was at Crookham, a straggling little village that takes its name from a sharp bend in the Till as it emerges from the Milfield plain and wriggles its way northward to join the Tweed, that there took place in 1678 what has sometimes been described as the last engagement of the Civil War. The Cheviots and the countryside round about them had long provided refuge for the Covenanters. At last the Privy Council could put up with them no longer, and ordered Colonel Strother of Fowberry to arrest their leader, John Welsh. In the ensuing scuffle, Strother's cousin Robert Marley was killed, as was Tom Ker of Hayhope, one of the Covenanters. The rest escaped, only to be indicted for murder, each side hailing its dead as a martyr.

To the east, and perched on a hill lined with trees, stands one of the show-places of Northumberland—Ford village—and the castle that guards the Ford over the Till from which the place takes its name.

It was in 1338 that Sir William Heron was given a licence to crenellate the manor house built in the previous century by Odinel de Forde; and one of the great castles of the Border was born. Of the 'quadrilateral' type, with a tower at each corner (two of which survive) it was destroyed in 1385 by the Scots, and again just before Flodden, while in 1549 it was once more battered by their artillery, though without success. Tradition has it that James IV spent his time here in dalliance with Lady Heron instead of continuing his march into England, and so gave Surrey the chance to bring him to battle at Flodden. Absolute nonsense; for in fact the poor lady was at that very moment with Surrey, imploring him to come to the rescue of her husband and castle.

Later on, Ford passed to the Delavals. It must have seemed a doubtful kind of inheritance, the land unenclosed and hardly a tree to be seen. With typical Delaval energy, however, they renovated the castle, in what has been unkindly described as Chippendale Gothic, and created an estate.

It was not, however, until it passed into the hands of the third Marquess of Waterford that the castle, and indeed the village, took on the appearance it has today. And all because he had married, in 1842, that astonishing female, Louisa, daughter of

Sir Charles Stuart, the British Ambassador in Paris. A woman of great energy as well as artistic talent, she proceeded, when her husband was killed some seventeen years later by a fall from his horse, to turn Ford from the somewhat uncouth place that she found it into her idea of an earthly paradise. First she rebuilt with the help of David Bryce, an Edinburgh architect, a good deal of the castle (now rented by the County Education Committee) in the baronial style affected by Victorians. Then she turned her attention to the village, pulling down most of the original (which was probably no loss) and rebuilding it among the beautiful trees and lawns of the castle grounds. At the west end stands what to modern eyes must seem a pretty hideous memorial to her husband, while the village itself consists of a couple of dozen Victorian Gothic houses in a warm golden stone. In the middle, opposite the best of the houses (the post office), stands the school with a couple of magnificent fig trees in front, and the chief tourist attraction of the place inside. These are the frescoes (which aren't frescoes at all but watercolours on paper) of biblical characters and scenes, which Lady Waterford painted herself. The models for the figures are mostly village people; the painting—in the Renaissance style—excellent, though alas, they are now beginning to deteriorate.

There is no doubt that this model village is pretty as a picture, with its neatly mown grass and profusion of roses, and would not be out of place somewhere in the home counties along with Letchworth and Welwyn Garden City. One must admit, however, that it really looks a bit strange in a county where history and climate have bred a tradition of massive buildings and rough grey stone.

To appreciate this one has only to turn to St Michael's church, built in the thirteenth century, and with one of those splendidly stark bell-cots perched on a buttress like a chimney breast, as at Felton and Bothal. Or the tower in which the vicars of Ford were once accustomed to find refuge. Now only its vaulted basement remains, with nine-foot-thick walls providing a tiny barbican between outer and inner doors, roofed with stone joists to withstand the reivers' unpleasant habit of 'scumfishing' the occupants—in other words smoking them out by piling wet straw against the entrance.

A mile or so downstream, past the gates of the castle's West

Lodge with their handsome bronze horses, is the ford itself (now crossed by a suitable bridge). Also, and now used as one of the estate buildings, the famous forge, one of the last in England to use water as a source of power and enjoying an enviable reputation for the spades it turned out. Nearby stands Heatherslaw Mill on a site which has been in use for 700 years. Mercifully the water wheel and most of the machinery remain intact, so that it has been found possible to renovate it as a working museum piece.

Northwards again, and one comes to Etal, the *halh* or Haugh where Eata lived. In two respects, at least, this is the counterpart of Ford. To begin with, it is the proud possessor of what was once a famous Border castle. Standing on a steep bank at the end of the village, commanding another of the Till fords, it was built, like Ford, in the mid-fourteenth century (for Sir Robert de Manners, an ancestor of the present Dukes of Rutland) and probably by the same masons. It never really recovered from the battering it received from James IV when he invaded England on behalf of Perkin Warbeck, and not much is now left standing, though the gate-house is still an impressive sight.

At the other end of the village street stands Etal Manor, a pleasant Georgian house of two storeys. Of the parish church of St Mary which stands in the manor grounds, perhaps the less said the better. Its principal claim to fame lies in its having been built and endowed by the widow of one of the natural children of William IV—Lady Augusta Fitzclarence.

Like Ford, moreover, this is a model village designed as an entity—and a very pleasant one it is. It consists of a single wide street lined with trees and flanked with stone cottages, most of them whitewashed and roofed with heavy dark slate which has replaced (with the exception of the 'Black Bull' and perhaps a couple of other houses) the original thatch. The whole provides a return to the Northumbrian tradition that I cannot help feeling is infinitely preferable to the south-country smugness of Ford. An opinion that seems to be shared by many, judging from the popularity of the ford as a picnicking place. Here children are to be seen 'plodging' by the remains of the bridge over which the captured Scottish artillery was brought after Flodden.

12

Norham and Islandshire

UNTIL quite recently the local authority responsible for the extreme north of Northumberland rejoiced in the resounding title of Norham and Islandshire, and it was its task to administer the two districts that for hundreds of years had, together with Bedlingtonshire, formed part of the domains of the Prince Bishops of Durham, who ruled them almost as an independent state. Ever since the lands that had been given by St Oswald to Lindisfarne Priory passed into their hands, the latter had been the greatest landowners in the north. It would have been easy to say the greatest in the county, but this could be confusing, for St Cuthbert's Land, as these three shires were originally known, was not considered until 1844 as being part of Northumberland at all, being known instead as North Durham.

The capital of the northernmost shire was, of course, Norham. Once known as Ubbanford (Ubba's Ford), its name was changed to the North Settlement, or Norham, to distinguish it from Durham itself. It was here that the Bishop, like any other independent prince, held his exchequer. In other words, his Chancellor would sit at the chequer-board used to demonstrate to the illiterate the calculations he made in accepting their rents and other payments. Here, also, Bishop Hugh Puiset began the magnificent castle that replaced an earlier one of Bishop Ranulf Flambard, destroyed by the Scots in 1136, or thereabouts.

Although a ruin, enough of the castle has been preserved to show how it was gradually strengthened through the years to keep up with the advances in siege tactics, and how it was repaired after the heavy battering it received before Flodden. Now, surrounded by fine beeches, it still stands proudly among the grass lawns and terraces that so enhance the beauty of the masonry. You can see the sheep gate where the villagers' stock was brought into the bailey when an attack was imminent, the pit (now filled in) into which the pivoting drawbridge once dipped, and the tunnel that brought the water from the mill burn in order to flood the moat.

Here, in 1318, Sir Thomas Grey was besieged for a year; again the next year for seven months, once more in 1322 and finally (and successfully) in 1327. It was during the second of these sieges that there appeared a Lincolnshire knight, Sir William Marmion, who had been enjoined by his lady-love to take the helmet with a golden crest that she had given him "to the most dangerous place in Britain and there make it famous". Soon after his arrival a strong party of Scottish horse approached, and Grey suggested that this was a good opportunity to do exactly that. "Mount your horse," he said, "and spur him into the midst of your enemies yonder. I forswear God if I rescue not thy body, dead or alive, or I myself will die for it." Whereupon Marmion mounted his horse, galloped out of what is still known as the Marmion Gate, and single-handed charged the Scots. Grey, meanwhile, issued out of another gate with the horsemen of the garrison, took the Scots in flank, rescued Marmion, who seems to have been little the worse for wear, and chased the attackers back across the River Tweed that runs so invitingly below.

It is as difficult to tear oneself away from the castle as it is to pass over the countless tales of Border warfare with which it has been associated. A descent past the lovely trees brings one, however, to the wide street and attractive little back lonnens of Norham itself. In the middle stands a village green surrounded by houses, some of which are whitewashed, some in their natural stone. Between them, they form a fitting background for a medieval market cross that consists of a tapering shaft rising out of a round, stepped base, the whole now topped by a weather-vane in the shape of a salmon. Once the village was almost entirely dependent on the salmon fisheries of the Tweed and there was a good deal of unemployment. Now, however, the industrial estate that has been created between East Ord and Berwick, as well as fresh jobs to be found at Coldstream, have restored the fortunes of the inhabitants, while a number of houses, modernized to suit the increased demand, have been changing hands at ever-increasing prices.

At the end of a tiny lonnen is the church which, in keeping with its origin, is dedicated to St Cuthbert. As befits such an important possession of the prince-bishopric of Durham, moreover, it looks like a young cathedral, marred only by an excruciating mid-eighteenth-century tower. Inside, the proportions are so good that one tends to forget its majestic size. There is a fine effigy of a crusading knight in the south wall of the chancel and a splendidly carved dark oak pulpit and stall brought from Durham Cathedral.

From quite early on there seems to have been a requirement for a large number of priests at Norham—perhaps because of the violent nature of the Borderers—and in the fourteenth century room had to be found for six extra confessors. As time went on, the fact that, as at Simonburn, the parish church was located in the extreme corner of a vast area, led to the building all over the place of chapels of ease to reduce the parishioners' travelling, and this in turn brought a requirement for a number of curates and for their training within the diocese. The problem of their accommodation seems to have been solved by housing them over the stables that until quite recently adorned the yard of Norham vicarage.

As one travels west, the valley of the Tweed widens into a series of haughs through which the river peacefully meanders. This countryside provides some of the most fertile land in Britain, with crops as early, or earlier, as any to be found in the Tyne Valley sixty miles to the south. Known to the envious as the Garden of Eden, its big farms have been able, even in the hardest times, to weather the storm.

Cornhill is separated from Coldstream, and therefore from Scotland, by a fine five-arch bridge designed by Smeaton, the architect of the Eddystone Lighthouse; and the tollhouse on the Scottish side has seen many a runaway marriage. The story goes that one celebrated statesman (why not mention him by name?) who had eloped with an heiress, was overtaken in Cornhill by the lady's guardian. Turning, he shot one of the leaders of his pursuer's chaise, and in the resultant confusion just found time to complete the marriage before his infuriated pursuer could stop him.

The village—whose name, incidentally, is quite unconnected with grain, but denotes the Hill where Cranes were to be found—consists of a single wide street with prim houses more reminiscent of Scotland than of England. One's first impression of the place on entering it from Norham is one of ancient and modern, in the shape of an old-fashioned smithy with, almost opposite it, a flourishing agricultural engineer's. On a peninsula formed by a sharp bend in the Tweed stands Collingwood House, a mansion of stone-flagged floors and grassy terraces, and at the junction of the Wark and Coldstream roads a fine coaching inn known as the 'Collingwood Arms'. It has been altered a good deal over the years and has lost (only temporarily, it is to be hoped) the choleric sign of an ancient Collingwood that used to hang there; however, it retains a couple of fine trees at the front.

Whereas Wark-on-Tyne derives its name from a man-made earthwork, Wark-on-Tweed takes its name from the Kaim, a curious ridge of gravel left by one of the glaciers that were once such a feature of this part of the country. Our ancestors may be forgiven for thinking this was also a work of man. Sixty feet high and fifty yards wide at the base, it slopes evenly upwards so that the top is only a yard wide and the whole looks like nothing so much as a railway embankment. At the east end it widens out into a knowe on which a few stones are virtually all that remain of another of the great fortresses of the Border. As famous in its own day as Norham, it had the added distinction of being, according to Froissart, the castle where Lady Salisbury dropped her garter and Edward III picked it up, quieting the courtiers' giggles with the immortal words, *"Honi soit qui mal y pense"*.

Below is still to be seen the remains of the bog that once formed part of the castle's defences, drained by a ditch known as the Goat's Mouth. To the west a little hillock by the roadside marks the spot where stood the castle gallows. The village itself is disappointing for, like the castle, it has all but disappeared; a few houses of no particular interest now represent a 'town' once famous throughout the country.

This is the extreme north-west corner of Northumberland, and only the tiny hamlet of Carham, the scene of a decisive battle in which, in 1018, the Scots wrested the Lothians from Northumberland, lies between us and the Border line where it leaves the Tweed.

There is only one course open, and that is to retrace our steps to Wark and Norham, and to renew acquaintance with the rolling cornfields and magnificent farm steadings—perhaps the finest in England—that are such a feature of north Northumberland. These are steadings where a couple of hundred cattle can be housed, and round which the farmer can walk to inspect them in his bedroom slippers if he should so wish, without even getting them dirty, and almost entirely under cover.

One's first glimpse of Duddo is what looks like a surprisingly complete tower standing on the bracken-covered crag that gave the place its name of Dudda's *hoh* or Heugh. Closer acquaintance reveals that it is but a mouldering shell. This was one of the towers that James was careful to destroy before Flodden. Rebuilt in Queen Elizabeth's time, its importance presumably diminished till it suffered the inevitable fate of such buildings, serving as a quarry for stone required elsewhere. The village itself is scarcely more than a hamlet, with a curious building turning out on closer acquaintance to be the church of St John, which was turned into a school when a fresh church was built outside the village.

A little way off the road that leads back to the Tweed at Horncliffe, lies something of a curiosity in the shape of Shoresdean. Here was built, not so many years ago, a settlement which was intended to provide for the old and the retired. Consisting of a hollow square of houses, with rather unpleasant curving roofs, surrounding a kind of village green, it has been supplied with a tiny sub-post office and no other amenities whatsoever. Linked to civilization by a rather uncertain bus service, it provides, in fact, an excellent illustration of how not, and where not, to build a village.

Horncliffe, built on a Horn, or Tongue, of land above a bend in the Tweed, is a very different kettle of fish. It begins with a smart-looking primary school, one of two in the district built to take the place of a number of the old-fashioned sort; followed by a council estate whose roofs point to its having been designed by the same council surveyor as Shoresdean. The village improves as it goes on, however, with a nice whitewashed house with a roof of red pantiles in the centre and the street widening out into a kind of square at the west end. This is as far as one can go, for the lovely dene, which houses an old mill, is difficult of access.

The ford here was one of the easiest on the lower reaches of the river and it is not surprising, therefore, that both Charles I and Oliver Cromwell camped at Horncliffe. Since 1820, however, there has been no need to use it, for in that year Captain Samuel Brown R.N. built the graceful Union Bridge, the first suspension bridge of any size in Britain.

Further down the river still lies the complex which begins with East Ord and continues as far as Berwick. At the former there is nothing much of note except the old mill (now converted to a dwelling house), a caravan park and the Berwick industrial estate. Between this and the Great North Road lie modern residential estates and, to the east of the road, Tweedmouth and Spittal.

Village, town or suburb? Despite the claims of each to be separate entities, a glance at the map shows what is indeed the case, that taken together they form for all practical purposes an extension of Berwick.

Travelling south, the first village after Tweedmouth is Scremer-ston, once the abode of some Norman worthy who perhaps was known as the Fencer (French *escrimeur*). For long enough the for-tunes of the place have depended on coal, though the good people of Berwick used not to be particularly enamoured of the business methods of those who worked the pit, complaining that they themselves were "very farr abused and evill intreated by such naughtye fellowes and servants as have the charge of the coale pitts of Skrymerstone" who were accustomed to giving "half a measure for holl* and serving countrymen and Scottesmen before any of the garrisons of the town". Time, however, has caught up with the offenders, for the colliery has had at last to close down. No longer can one walk into the Miners Arms and see fifty foaming glasses of beer lined up on the counter to await the men coming off shift, for the pitmen have all gone. Even the village itself has changed with the years, having gradually moved southward until the greater part of it now lies along the A1—and one of its fastest stretches at that. Only the smithy, complete with spreading chest-nut tree (or is it a hornbeam?), the church and vicarage, remain

* Whole.

among the modern houses to remind one of the time when the manor belonged to the Earls of Derwentwater, from which it passed, like the rest of their estates, into the keeping of Greenwich Hospital.

When the plague visited Scremerston in 1667, the sufferers were taken down to the nearby links and parked in huts made from the bents there, whereas now anyone mown down by the traffic presumably ends up in Berwick infirmary.

Another place to be decimated by the plague was Ancroft—the Single, or Lone Croft. Once this was quite a considerable place, with a clog-making industry that turned to making boots for Marlborough's army. On the south side of the little village, with its big farm and mostly modern houses, runs the Dean burn in a valley much too large for the job it has to do. The explanation is that it is believed to have once been that of the Till, until a glacier caused the river to change its course.

The way southwards leads up a hill known as the Bride's Brae, so called because at some time in the eighteenth century a girl riding up the hill to her wedding was thrown from her horse and killed. A rolling field to the left of the road is still known as the Broomie Huts, for here it was that the plague victims were carried, and a shelter of broom placed over them, bodies and broom being eventually burnt together. The line of trees that runs along the south side of the dene to the right of the road was planted in memory of the deaths, one tree for each clogger who died.

In Ancroft there stands another of those churches that served not only as a place of worship but as a refuge when the Scots were known to be on the way. This was made possible by blocking up, in the thirteenth or fourteenth century, the original Norman doorway, and making out of the west end of the church a flat-topped tower complete with walls some four feet thick, and a vaulted basement. The three floors above, together with the fireplace, have since been removed, as have some of the outbuildings of the vicarage next door, which, according to the plans put forward by the Archdeacon of the Diocese, originally "consisted . . . of a large edifice, capable of receiving 200 children, and . . . under the same roof a comfortable habitation for the curate".

Bowsden, a little further to the south, lies on the slope of a Hill where some kind of *botl*, or Building, once stood. It is not so long since it consisted of three farms and a tiny pub, and nothing much else. The 'Black Bull', a funny old-fashioned little place, whitewashed and red-tiled, survives pretty well unchanged, but many of the cottages, as well as the school, have been spruced up to accommodate outsiders, and new bungalows seem to spring up almost at will.

There is quite a sharp difference between the appearance of the houses on the west of the Milfield plain and those on the east, the former being built of the local volcanic stone, but the latter of either sandstone or limestone. It is the presence of this limestone that distinguishes the countryside round Lowick; a land of rolling cornfields and strange lumpy hollows grown over with grass, that is not strictly speaking part of Islandshire, but close enough to warrant its inclusion in this chapter. These hollows are almost all that is now to be seen of the quarries which used to produce the stone that, with the aid of local coal, was burnt into lime not only for local use but for an export trade on which the prosperity of Lowick—the Farm on the tiny River Low—was founded. The faulted nature of the coal seams finally made them uneconomic to work and the lime industry died, leaving Lowick to subsist as best it could on agriculture and forestry. Even the local brickworks have gone, though there have appeared a cluster of grain silos which the trade with Europe now demands.

That this was once a bigger and more prosperous centre than it can ever pretend to be now is emphasized by the fact that, quite apart from the meeting house of the Plymouth Brethren at nearby Barmoor, there were until quite recently no less than four churches and chapels here. As one enters the village from Bowsden, the gloomy C. of E. church with its steep-roofed tower greets one; followed by a much pleasanter-looking Catholic church, one wing of which forms a church hall, the other (providing an unfortunate advertisement for the local brick) the presbytery. The Methodist chapel is now a shop, but fronting the village green which forms part of a kind of suburb to the south, where once the Devil's Causeway ran, stands the United Reformed church. Opposite is a house that was once the miller's. When the mill stream suddenly vanished into the limestone workings, the mill carried on with steam, but finally gave up the unequal struggle. The remains of a Border tower or bastle are to be found among the farm buildings in the centre of the village. At Bastle Corner, next door, is a large edifice, once a granary, and now converted into a dwelling house, with a pleasant Georgian doorway. In front of this is the tiny green where the farm 'hirings' used to take place each March, but which is now set off by a dignified war memorial.

Back into Islandshire, it is no great distance to Beal (the Bee Hill from which the monks of Holy Island drew their honey) and the causeway which takes one over the channel that leads to the island itself. But only for a few hours at a time, for the water comes right over the road when the tide rises. So much so that there is provided a refuge like a crow's-nest, into which the unwary may climb; but their car would have to take care of itself, and it is not unknown for the occasional visitor who has taken a chance to get himself (or herself) drowned. There seems no doubt that the name Lindisfarne denotes the Island of those who Fare to and from Lindsey—that is to say North Lincolnshire—but why this should be, no one has ever explained. One thing, however, is certain, that in the 'season' too many people these days fare— not only from Lincolnshire but from all over Britain, to have a look at this cradle of English Christianity—for Holy Island village to accommodate. Every little street and road around the place is jam-packed with parked cars, and walking becomes suicidal.

Yet once this was just a fishing village with virtually no other outlet for the islanders' energies. "The Holy Islande", runs a fourteenth-century description, "is situated within the sea [it would be surprising if it were not!] . . . and hath in the same a little borough towne all sete with fishers very poor."

It is a curious jumble, this place, with no apparent rhyme or reason, and this is really its great attraction. It looks as if the inhabitants had taken seriously the adage of "something old, something new, something borrowed, something blue," and just plumped down a house wherever the builder thought fit, one, at least, suffering the indignity of an asbestos roof.

The island has always been an object of pilgrimage. Here it was that St Aidan came from Iona, at the request of King Oswald, to found a see and monastery. Here also, in 664, came St Cuthbert the shepherd boy who for a dozen years was Bishop of Lindisfarne before he retired to a cell in the Farne Islands. Almost in the village itself stand the remains of the Norman priory begun in

1080. One can still trace, with the aid of the illustrated guide, where the various buildings stood, and even get some idea of how the monks lived in this outpost of religion. Best of all, one can stand at the western end and enjoy in the old arches of the priory church, and the pillars so reminiscent of Durham Cathedral, one of the most beautiful sights in Northumberland.

Between priory and village there stands the parish church of St Mary. Built in the thirteenth century, it possesses another of those delightful buttressed bell-cots (though the top part has been renewed) and a chancel that, like the older priory church, has sides which slope outwards as they get higher, giving a fortress-like appearance from inside. On show is a copy of the marvellously illuminated Lindisfarne Gospel, the original of which is in the British Museum.

Separated a little way from the village and its tiny harbour is the astonishing little castle perched, for all the world like a child's toy, on a rock at the seaward end of the island. Originally built as a protection against the Scots, from stone filched from the priory at the Dissolution of the Monasteries, it has since been restored and made habitable by Sir Edwin Lutyens.

May is probably the best time of year at which to visit Holy Island village, when life is proceeding more or less normally, and the villagers can gather once more in the Reading Room or at Sally's (now Sally's Gift Shop), or the cockpit facing St Cuthbert's Island. It is then also that one can enjoy a peaceful pint in the 'Iron Rails' (now re-hashed and without the rails that gave it its name). Or eat fresh salmon sandwiches in the 'Northumberland Arms', where the certificates awarded to George Kyle, the coxswain of the Holy Island lifeboat, compete with photographs of the Newcastle United team who were expected to win the 1973 Cup and didn't. Or, far from the madding crowd, contemplate the religious atmosphere and curious overtones of a place that is like no other in England.

L

13

Bamburghshire

WHAT our ancestors would have described as "the chiefest town" in the old Bamburgh ward has always been Belford, a place whose meaning no one seems able to define with certainty but which was certainly called after the Ford in the burn now known by the same name. And probably after the Crag which sticks up in what may well have been a marsh, and which now supports St Mary's church. Whether, in fact, it is a town rather than a village is another matter altogether, but its atmosphere is sufficiently that of the latter to warrant its inclusion in this book.

In the days when constant invasion had so recently made it a waste of time to build any habitation other than of stone six or eight feet thick, it is hardly surprising that a traveller in the reign of Charles I could still describe this as "the most miserable beggarly town, or town of sods, that was ever made in an afternoon of loam and sticks. In all the town not a loaf of bread, nor a quart of beer, nor a lock of hay, nor a peck of oats, and little shelter for horse or man." Since then, however, its establishment as a post town, straddling the Great North Road, has led to an increase both in size and in accommodation for travellers. In the early days of the last century, for instance, there were no fewer than six inns as well as a brewery (which must in these circumstances have been a very paying proposition) and a weaving shop. Since then, though the village has lost some of these amenities, it has gained a station on the main Edinburgh line, with a cattle mart beside it; a fine United Reformed church, a Methodist chapel, a village hall which at the time of writing is having a dance floor added above it, and even one or two factories.

Once there were nearly two thousand inhabitants but, with the depopulation common to all the countryside, this number must have declined considerably. No less than fifty of the men-folk were killed in the 1914–18 war; a body blow if ever there was one. Since then a couple of council housing estates have been added, and it is hoped that the presence of the new factories will halt the population drain.

But it is the coaching tradition that has long been the life-blood of Belford, and one that has never really died out, its most noticeable feature still being the Blue Bell Hotel which dominates the little market place. Rising to fame in the old days under the management of Elizabeth Macdonald and after her, a Mrs Henderson, it still provides an attractive stopping place for travellers to and from Scotland.

As you travel up the Great North Road towards Belford, past the great farmsteads of South Charlton and North Charlton, there lies a mile or so to the east of the road the tiny village of Ellingham. The Hall is no longer inhabited by the Haggerstons, who have been in these parts since Norman times, and at Ellingham since 1698, but by a preparatory school. Nowadays the place is just a pleasant little backwater, but it was not always thus. Not only are the Haggerstons staunch Catholics but, not unnaturally perhaps, they were staunch Jacobites as well. When Butcher Cumberland was on his way to Scotland to quell the Forty-five rebellion, Sir Carnaby Haggerston, the third baronet, was required to send his coach and horses to convey him from Belford to Berwick. Finding himself in a dilemma whether to refuse and endanger his family, or to accede and further a cause to which he was opposed, he solved the problem by bribing his coachman to overturn the vehicle on the way. When, later on, he was bidden to supply transport for the baggage of Cumberland's troops, he went one better and moved all his horses to another of his estates. No wonder that his memorial in St Maurice's church (which serves the Protestants of the parish, as distinct from the Catholic chapel that forms part of the Hall) describes him not only as "a Gentleman of uncommon erudition" but "of clear and penetrating wit and solid judgment".

On the way from Ellingham to Bamburgh lies the sleepy little village of Lucker. Now the Scandinavians, although they made sporadic raids on the coast of Northumberland, provided a dynasty of Northumbrian earls, and influenced to a marked degree the language that we speak, affected very little the placenames of the county. Lucker is an exception to this rule, for the name is Old Scandinavian for a Swamp frequented by Sandpipers! Little more than a mile away stands Adderstone Hall, the ancestral home for long enough of the Forsters, of whom we shall hear more in a moment.

The passage of time hardly seems to have affected Lucker over the last century or so. The mill, however, has become a farmhouse and the school a youth centre, where children competing for the Duke of Edinburgh awards, or engaged in other country pursuits, can stay. The station, on the main London–Edinburgh line, has been closed, but a caravan site adds a little life to the village, and the little Apple Inn soldiers on.

And now for Bamburgh, a place so packed with history that one is tempted to paraphrase the historian of Haydon Bridge and write "I can only say that as my pen approaches the subject, I find it all too overwhelming". It all begins with the castle, towering majestic on a rock that is part of the Great Whin Sill that stretches across Northumberland from the Roman Wall to the Farne Islands. A quarter of a mile long and rising 150 feet above the sands, it is, and always has been, a remarkable defensive position. It is no surprise, therefore, to discover that it was fortified by the Ancient Britons, by whom it was known as Dinguardi, meaning the Citadel of the Games, or that it has therefore been identified as the Joyous Garde of Arthurian Legend.

Here in 547 King Ida, the Flamebearer, created in wood the first capital of Bernicia which, when his grandson Ethelfrith bequeathed it to his widow, finally became known as Bebba's Burgh, and hence Bamburgh. In Norman times it was rebuilt in stone, since when it was never captured, despite frequent attempts during the Wars of the Roses, until the Royalists, under Sir Ralph Grey, took it in 1644, only to find themselves besieged in turn and the castle battered down over their heads.

By then it had passed into the hands of the Forsters of Adderstone, who, being already a good deal down on their luck, sold it, with the rest of the Forster estates, to Lord Crewe. The Lord Crewe Trust, in turn, sold the castle to the first Lord Armstrong, the great engineer, who completed its restoration. It is now let as flats.

The centre of Bamburgh is built round a triangular green, grown up with fair-sized trees, and known as the Grove. Thence the Wynding leads down to the seaside villas, to the site of the old lifeboat station, to a fine golf-course among the sandhills, and finally to the sea. Northwards lie the rocks from which the ill-intentioned have been known to pot with rifles at the eider duck, known after St Cuthbert (who befriended them) as Cuddy's chickens. To the south lie the sands which, backed, as they are, by the majestic castle, have provided the setting for many a film scenario.

Facing one side of the Grove stand three notable hostelries in the shape of the 'Lord Crewe Arms', the 'Victoria' and the 'Castle Inn', while on the seaward side stands the manor house of the Forsters, built in 1692, and a magnificent cruciform church, its effect enhanced by carefully mown lawns. There is a fine squint that looks more like an unglazed window at the south-west corner of the church, and on the north wall a memorial to Thomas Forster, who led the Northumbrians in the Fifteen, and to other members of his family, set up by Dorothy, Lady Crewe. Beyond that is another tablet, by the side of which hang the helmet, breast-plate and gauntlets that historians ascribe to Ferdinando Forster. They look as if they must already have been pretty old-fashioned in 1701 when Ferdinando was killed by John Fenwick of Rock in a brawl in the streets of Newcastle. In fact the church is full of memorials, including one marking the spot where traditionally St Aidan (after whom the church is named) died in 651.

It is not the Forsters however—who were really rather a dull and uninspiring lot—that have made Bamburgh a place of pilgrimage, for the whole place has become a kind of shrine to Grace Darling, with a Grace Darling Museum which shows every conceivable and inconceivable relic of her life, a hideous memorial in the churchyard, and reminders of her everywhere you go.

Time passes and heroines, as much as heroes, tend to be debunked; but Grace Darling's fame lives on. Born in 1817, the daughter of a lighthouse keeper, she spent the first twenty-one years of her life on the Longstone, one of the Farne Islands which lie opposite Bamburgh. She grew up in a tough environment, and there was probably little else for her and her brother George to do but learn how to handle a boat and to help their father. One day in September 1838 the steamer *Forfarshire* was making for Dundee from Hull with a cargo of machinery, when a tremendous storm blew up. Unable to enter the harbour at Berwick, the captain turned southward again and, failing to pick up the warning light, struck the dreaded Harker rocks, and the ship began to break up. Nine of the crew and a single passenger got away in a boat and were picked up exhausted. Forty-three passengers were swept away and drowned, leaving the rest clinging perilously to the fore-part, which was jammed in the rocks. When dawn came Grace spotted the survivors and told her father. There was only one course open to them, for father and daughter to launch the heavy coble and battle their way through the mountainous seas, in the hope that in the unlikely event of their being able to reach the survivors they would be in good enough shape to help in rowing the coble back. When they reached what was left of the ship, it became clear that the boat would be dashed to pieces if it approached any closer, Father scrambled through the breakers while daughter kept the coble within reach, and eventually they managed to rescue four men and the solitary woman. Then two of the rescued crewmen accompanied William Darling back and brought off the remaining four men—all that were left.

The whole story has become so much a part of the folk-lore of Northumberland that it has almost ceased to amaze. At the time, however, Grace Darling was the toast of England, and rightly so, for the sheer physical strength required to row a coble in heavy seas, let alone the danger, marks the girl who now lies in peace in Bamburgh as a heroine of no mean order.

If you really want to see cobles—the modern equivalent of the Viking ships—at work, you should go to Seahouses some five miles further south along the dunes. In the days when this was just a de-lightful little fishing port, it was salmon that brought in the money but, since fishing for salmon has been restricted, lobstering and (insofar as the wives can still be persuaded to bait the hooks) a little 'long-lining', have pretty well taken its place.

Perhaps it was when Ubbanford changed its name to Norham—the North Settlement of the Bishops of Durham—that the village now known as North Sunderland was first known as Suthelande (the Southern Land). Then, for some inexplicable reason the name acquired another 'land' at the end and became Sutherlannland. Presumably this came to be pronounced as Sunderland and to be confused with the town of that name, so that 'North' was added in an attempt to make a further distinction; thus completing a process which must have few equals for etymological idiocy.

It was when North Sunderland, then, as now, a pleasant if undistinguished village with a number of good pubs, was connected to the main line at Chathill, that "North Sunderland Seahouses" began to develop from just a flourishing fishing port into a popular resort.

Things have now gone so far that one wonders what N.S. must think of this cuckoo that it has nurtured. Bingo halls, pin tables, self-service restaurants, gift shops and all the fun of the fair have now beset Seahouses, which is rapidly becoming a miniature Blackpool. Furthermore, although it may not boast a tower it can provide something that neither Blackpool, Brighton nor Weston-super-Mare can rival, and that is the boat trip to the Farne Islands, for which queues of visitors form up all through the season, to be taken to what is now a bird sanctuary, inhabited by eider duck and Arctic tern, and surrounded by seals.

When the craze began for messing about in boats it was not altogether easy on the exposed coast of Northumberland to find a stretch of sea suitable for the learner in his dinghy. In the end it was Beadnell Bay that came nearest to filling the bill, and with it came a new lease of life for the quiet little village that had started out as the Low Ground by the sea where Beda lived.

The village proper lies some half a mile from the harbour. A large building estate and a caravan park in the grounds of what is now the Beadnell Hall Hotel do little to reduce the attraction of the older part. In Beadnell Hall are two panelled rooms forming part of a Georgian extension, whose outside dimensions do not agree with those within: yet no one seems to have found out how to obtain access to the space in between. There is also an odd-looking pub in the shape of the 'Craster Arms', which displays, as an embellishment, the coat of arms of the Crasters of Craster, with their motto "While there's life there's hope". Still standing three storeys high, it is in fact a spruced-up Border tower, originally built by the same Forsters whom we have already met at

Blanchland and Bamburgh, with walls eight feet thick and the usual vaulted basement, now used as a beer cellar.

From the tiny harbour the fishing cobles still go out in search of lobsters, though the production of kippers is no more. Nor, so far as one knows, is the smuggling for which Beadnell used to be famous (or infamous, if you prefer it). Now serving as a majestic background for the pleasure craft that infest the beach are the remains of the lime kilns that used to be such a feature of the place. So much so that in the eighteenth century it was found necessary to enlarge and improve the tiny harbour to cope with the coastal trade in lime burnt here and elsewhere.

At the southern end of the bay which gives such pleasure to dinghy sailors and holidaymakers lies Newton-by-the-Sea, which can best be described as a couple of separate hamlets rather than as a single village. First comes Newton Hall and the tiny village green and pleasant little pub which, along with a few houses, make up High Newton-by-the-Sea, which is not by the sea at all. Then, after about a mile, Low Newton which really is by the sea, and which finishes up as Newton Square, a little suburb built round another green and graced by a friendly pub called 'The Ship'.

Part of the attraction of Low Newton is that it is the deadest of ends. To continue south therefore, you have to retrace your steps somewhat and pass through Embleton, the Hill, believe it or not, once infested by Caterpillars. It is not for caterpillars, however, that the village has since become famous, so much as for the magnificence of near-by Dunstanburgh Castle on its rocky headland overlooking Queen Margaret's Cove, and for the erudition of its vicars. Dunstanburgh, unfortunately, is outside the scope of this book; not so the parsons who, in the intervals of serving the fourteenth-century church, seem to have wielded a nifty pen. Here, for instance, in the reign of Queen Anne, lived the Reverend Richard Parker, a cousin of Steele the essayist, who wrote the famous *Cure for a Scold* and made himself very unpopular by commenting in a letter to the *Spectator* on the manners and conversation of the local squirearchy. He was succeeded by one Tovey who wrote *The History and Antiquities of the Jews in England*. Another of the same sort was William Bolland, a classicist and theologian, while the best known of the lot was Mandell Creighton, afterwards Bishop of London, a friend of the Greys at nearby Fallodon and Howick, and especially of Sir Edward Grey who was to become Foreign Secretary. It was in the vicarage here that Creighton wrote *The History of the Papacy* and the *Life of Sir George Grey*, as well as helping to collect material for the Northumberland County History. Perhaps it was the influence of Merton College, Oxford, in whose gift the living remains, that ensured this succession of literary parsons. Or was it the peaceful atmosphere of the village, and particularly of the vicarage, that inspired them? For here, attached to the house, is one of those typically Northumbrian delights, a vicar's peel, with its vaulted basement and corkscrew stair, while near at hand stand two aged dovecots, one in brick with a penthouse roof, the other in stone, shaped rather like a beehive. The theory that it may have been the environment that had such a potent effect is reinforced by the fact that W. T. Stead, the reforming journalist who was eventually drowned in the *Titanic*, was born in the manse of the United Reformed church here.

Nowadays Embleton is quite a big place, for only a mile from the centre of the village lies Embleton Bay with its sheltered sands, along which runs the Dunstanburgh Castle golf-course, and it has become a resort both for holidaymakers and for those who indulge in weekend and summer cottages. It is a village of short streets criss-crossing each other, of good-sized pubs such as the old-fashioned Bluebell Inn and the much grander Dunstanburgh Hotel, and of a village hall, said to be the largest in the county, that was erected in memory of Bishop Creighton.

Further inland lies the little hamlet of Rock, the very model of a self-contained estate village. At one end stands the Hall (now a youth hostel) with a fifteenth-century tower that once housed a band of the Spanish mercenaries who, like their fellows from elsewhere, were to prove such a menace to friend and foe in their defence of the Border. Once Rock belonged to the Salkelds, and in the little Norman church there is a memorial to "a truly valiant and loyal gentleman, Col. John Salkeld, who served King Charles I with a constant, dangerous and expensive loyalty". It is hardly to be expected that it would further refer to the fact that in his youth he had fallen upon John Swinburne of Capheaton in a drunken passion and stabbed him to death. In some mysterious way he seems to have avoided hanging, became a magistrate and lived to be eighty-nine. The estate subsequently passed into the hands of the Fenwicks, but there must have been something in the air that incited its owners to violence, for was it not a Fenwick of Rock who murdered Ferdinando Forster?

Among some splendid trees bordering a village green is an ornamental pond, and opposite it a line of charming stone cottages and the old school. Don't be misled by the date over the door. If you look more closely you will find that the inscription reads "1623 T.S./A.S. Rebuilt 1855 RBB/CB". The first initials are of course those of the current Salkelds; the second those of the Bosanquets, a Huguenot family who still own the estate.

At Rennington there once lived Regna's People, one of whom (in fact Regna's son) was among the bearers of St Cuthbert's coffin when the monks of Holy Island fled from the marauding Danes to Durham. Nowadays it is a pleasant, rather dull little place with a pub, a school, a farm or two and a church with an unpleasant tower.

It is not so long ago that Craster—the old Encampment inhabited by Crows—was just a small fishing village belonging, like Craster Tower, a little distance inland, to the family of that name who have been there since goodness knows when. It was in 1906 that they built the tiny harbour for the export to different parts of the country of the whinstone slabs for which their quarries were famous. When you mention Craster to a Northumbrian, however, or for the matter of that to a lot of other people—particularly if they are fond of their food—they will reply "Oh, yes. Kippers." And they will be right, for these are the finest in the land, and supplied to the Queen herself. Fresh herring ("caller harn" as the old fishwives used to call them) landed by the local cobles, or brought in from North Shields, are split, soaked in brine and then hung in racks over a slow fire of chips and sawdust (preferably oak). Eat them that same evening, and Craster kippers are fit for a king, as indeed they are for a queen.

Take away the visitors who infest the place during the summer months, and forget the souvenirs in the shops, and you are left with an atttractive fishing village that hides its council houses away at its southern end, and boasts such delightful pubs as the 'Jolly Fisherman' (near the kippering sheds) and the 'Chough'.

Old towers seem two-a-penny in and around Craster. One of

them, which appears in the record of 1415, is incorporated with a lot of neo-Gothic in Craster Tower itself: the remains of another are to be found included in that glorious jumble known with fine impartiality as Proctors Stead or Dunstan Hall. It is rare indeed to find in Northumberland a house, as distinct from a tower or castle, that is much more than three hundred years old but here is one which, in part, is so ancient that no one seems to know quite when it began. Bits of it certainly go back to the thirteen-hundreds, if not earlier; part of it with its mullioned windows to the fifteenth century; other parts to 1706 and 1831; while the north wing, of old stone from elsewhere, was added in 1939 when the rest was restored. The oldest part is the red-roofed tower, and it is claimed as the birthplace in 1265 of the famous scholar and philosopher Duns Scotus. The inhabitants of Duns in Berwickshire also claim him, but it is difficult to ignore his own manuscript, preserved in the library of Merton College, in which he writes "Here endeth the lecture of . . . John Duns, who was born in a certain hamlet of the parish of Emylton, called Dunstan, in the county of Northumberland," and his education by the Grey Friars of Newcastle.

South again, and you reach Long Houghton (pronounced Hoeton) the Homestead on the Heugh or Spur of a Hill, that appears in 1241 as Magna Houcton. Straggling along what was once an important road from Alnmouth to Bamburgh, it includes at its northern end a mass of new houses, some of which are the married quarters of the officers, some of the men, of the RAF who man the radar and other installations nearby. The houses are divided into terraces named after various RAF celebrities and in their midst stands a splendid NAAFI canteen.

It has long been a source of irritation that farm workers occupy in so many cases cottages which go with the job, and which they must leave when they move to another farm, or retire. Contrariwise, as Tweedledee would say, it is impossible to run a farm unless the farmer can be sure of accommodation for his workers. It is important therefore that there should be somewhere to which they can retire, and in Long Houghton are to be found a number of suitable bungalows owned by the Robertson Trust, which was set up for exactly this purpose.

At the east end of the village is the church, and a little village green with a substantial stone house that used once to be the Bluebell Inn. Unfortunately there were certain villagers who, when they patronized this establishment on Sunday mornings, were to be seen capering about on the green when the more devout issued forth from morning service. Accordingly the Duchess of the day (the village, like so many others, belongs to the Duke of Northumberland) ordained that the pub should be closed, and closed it was.

It is St Peter's church, however, with its squat, massive tower, that is the most interesting feature of Long Houghton. Just inside the churchyard stands a tombstone on which is carved what looks like Mrs Neptune standing by an anchor which apparently floats on the waves, one hand on her hip, the other propping up her chin. It commemorates the master of a brig who was drowned with all his crew off Dunstanburgh Castle in 1847. Clarkson, in his survey of 1567, reported that, in the absence of a peel nearby, "the church and steple is the great strength that the poor tenants have to draw to in tyme of warre," and the evidence is still to be seen in the shape of slit windows and walls five feet thick. The incorporation of the tower with the church itself has exaggerated what is claimed to be the narrowest nave in the county.

In the late seventeenth century St Peter's was served by the Reverend George Duncan, whose pleasure it was to annotate the parish register with remarks (mercifully in Latin) regarding the character and habits of each parishioner. "A bad son of a bad father", "a quack and warlock doctor" and "a vile drunken female sinner" are only a few of the comments he made; though occasionally he relented a little with entries such as "very unhappily married" or "the best of wives".

Nearer the coast is to be found Boulmer Hall, a biggish farm with a set of delightful cottages and, a little further on, Boulmer itself. Pronounced 'Boomer', the place takes its name from the little natural haven which is supposed once to have been known as the Bullocks' Mere, but more likely the Mere where someone named Bulla (the Bullock) lived. Tradition has it that the inhabitants, like those of many of the fishing villages in Northumberland, are of Scandinavian rather than pure Anglian origin, and that, marrying very much among themselves, they have kept it that way.

The effect of this, so far as Boulmer is concerned, seems to have been twofold; first the size and weight of the fishermen compared to their neighbours, and second the reputation for smuggling that they used to enjoy, for they sent "brandy for the parson, baccy for the clerk" as far afield as Coquetdale and Glendale and over the border to Kelso. Twenty or thirty would ride in convoy as protection against the ambushes of the excisemen, and many are the tales told of such characters as Will Faw, the gipsy king of Yetholm, Cranstoun of Smailholm (who should have known better)

And Bob Dunn o' the Forest,*
He's riding te Boomer for gin,
Wi' three famed horses fra' Bushy Gap Lonnen
But 'Kate o' the West' is the Queen o' them aa'.

It is a plain and unassuming little hamlet, with a row of fishermen's cottages facing the sea, a few rather newer houses and a tiny church. Tools of the fishermen's trade are to be seen everywhere, including the cobles and the tractor that pulls them up the shore. If you are lucky, you may arrive just as one of the boats comes in with its cargo and you can buy a salmon (or better still, because of the delicacy of its flavour, a salmon trout) straight out of the sea. Ever since 1825 there has been a lifeboat here, and many are the tales of heroism connected with it. In the little pub called the 'Fishing Boat' is a striking painting that shows the women of Boulmer, as was their custom, dragging the lifeboat along the dunes in order to save the strength of their men in rowing it to wherever it was required. Now, alas, the RNLI have withdrawn the boat. So convinced was the village, however, of the necessity to safeguard its fishing fleet, and go to the help of the amateur yachtsmen who get into difficulties that, with the help of the people of the district, they have bought a high-speed motorboat to serve much the same purpose.

From Boulmer inland again to Lesbury, the Manor of the Leech or Physician. There is a great similarity in the villages built on the Duke's estates, and the neat gabled houses here are altogether typical. It is a long, wandering, largely one-sided village with plenty of trees, a fine medieval bridge over the Aln, and a nice church with a good deal of Norman work in it and a tower with a

* Rothbury forest.

pyramidical top. Among a series of notable vicars the Reverend Patrick Mackilwyan stands out. Beginning with a ferocious row with the villagers over tithes, he finally redeemed himself during the plague of 1665. This was one of the places where the afflicted were taken out onto the moor and left to die under makeshift tents, and the vicar earned his parishioners' regard by visiting the dying regardless of the danger. Ninety-seven at the time, he survived until he was a hundred and one, when he declared that "of friends and books, good and few are best," and died.

If you are travelling to Edinburgh by train, or indeed pursuing the coast road to the north, one of the most delightful views you are likely to see will be the red roofs and occasional whitewashed walls of Alnmouth, on the far side of the Aln estuary. In medieval times Alemouth, as it was spelt (and until recently, pronounced) was a port of considerable importance; the original borough, then known like so many other places as Newbiggin, being founded by William de Vesci, Lord of Alnwick, by virtue of a deed executed in Edinburgh at the court of William the Lion. (It was Herbert Honeyman, I think, who once lamented that Northumberland had not continued part of Scotland). In the days when the county was one of the granaries of England, it was from Alnmouth that a great deal of its grain was exported to more needy parts of the country and, for all I know, to the Continent. So much so that in the improving days of the eighteenth century a number of landowners clubbed together to construct the 'Corn Road', which we have already come across on its way from Hexham north-eastwards through Rothbury and Alnwick, in order to bring grain to the granaries here.

To John Wesley, who arrived in 1748, the place appeared as "a small sea-port town famous for all kinds of wickedness". No doubt he would have regarded it as just retribution when thirty years later the place suffered bombardment by the famous pirate, Paul Jones. A far cry indeed from 684 when there was held here the great synod that chose Cuthbert to be bishop of Lindisfarne.*

Since then a good deal of water has come down the Aln, so much so in fact that in 1806 the river broke through the isthmus at its mouth and left the hill, on which the successor to the old

* Or was Whittingham really the "place of two fords" mentioned by Bede?

Saxon church of St Waleric stood, completely cut off from the village. To those with evil memories of St Valery-en-Caux in the Second World War, St Waleric's name may well strike a chord. Now nothing of his church or its Norman successor remains—nor indeed of the harbour or its granaries—while only a small boat-yard and a few yachts and sailing dinghies survive to remind one of a once-flourishing coastal trade.

Yet the shape of the village itself must have changed little, for the outlines of its medieval predecessor can still be traced, and the broad high street that is now distinguished by the whitewash and black paint of the Schooner Hotel and the comfortable stone of the smaller 'Red Lion', runs pretty well where it always did. Along the seashore stretches a golf-course which disputes with Blackheath the honour of being the oldest golf-course in England after West-ward Ho!, while at Foxton Hall, on the high ground above the village, there is to be found another. Pleasant as they are, these are only two of the amenities that have made Alnmouth such a delightful place for a holiday, particularly for children, and a splendid haven for retirement.

A little way inland, one comes upon the ridge of Shilbottle where, for some reason, the People of Shipley (near Alnwick) once had a Dwelling, so that the place became known as Shiplingbotl. Before that there had been a British settlement there, approached by a causeway, while in more recent times the place has grown and multiplied almost with abandon.

A survey of the Percy estates made in 1567 stated that "there is within these fields of Shilbottle one coal mine which is much profitable for the tenants there and for the inhabitants of the towns thereabouts", and coal has always played an important part in the fortunes of the village. Since then it has been a colliery near Bilton (to the north-east of the village itself) that has worked the seam that was "much profitable for the tenants", and for long enough part of the village known as Shilbottle Grange has been devoted to the houses of pitmen employed there. Soon after the First World War the Co-operative Wholesale Society, of all people, sank a new pit at Shilbottle Woodhouse, and the Bilton colliery subsequently ceased work. All these comings and goings, together with the likelihood that the Shilbottle seam will be worked for many years to come, have naturally affected very considerably the size and nature of the village. The most widely used road, that from the A1 to Alnmouth, runs through the older part, and leaves one in blissful ignorance that anything more exists, apart from the church whose tower is to be seen peeping through the trees to the south. In point of fact there are two quite distinct sections of the old village, separated not so much by a village green as by a rectangular field. To the east, furthermore, lies Shilbottle Grange, with its large modern school and streets of modern houses. To the west is the council estate to which pitmen and their families from Cumberland, and from Scremerston, were brought when their pits closed down, of whom the Cumbrians, at any rate, have integrated quite successfully with the locals and with the pitmen who were there before them. The result of it all is the presence of nearly three and a half thousand people in what remains a complex of villages rather than the town which its population might otherwise suggest.

In the south part of the old village stands the church of St James, with its white marble tablet from the Alhambra Palace at Granada that now commemorates Samuel Widdrington, Captain in the Royal Navy. (As with Lord Derwentwater, you simply can't get away from him!). On the wall of the vicarage, adjoining the churchyard, is a plaque inscribed with the last four lines of a verse from an inscription in Melrose Abbey, the original of which reads:

> The earth goeth on the earth
> Glistring like gold.
> The earth goes to the earth
> Sooner than it wold.
> The earth builds on the earth
> Castles and towers.
> The earth says to the earth
> All shall be ours.

No doubt one of the towers in question was that which was built, like so many others, as a defence against the Scots and, after appearing in the list of castles and towers drawn up in 1415, has been incorporated in the present vicarage, though there is no evidence that it was specifically intended for the vicar. That some form of protection was definitely needed is apparent from the account we have of Mark Ker of Cessford promising the Earl of

The 'Black Bull' at Etal

The 'Black Bull' at Bowsden

Lowick: the old granary at Bastle Corner

The market cross, Norham

Luncheon time in Belford

Bamburgh: the Manor House of the Forsters

In the shadow of Bamburgh Castle

(*below*) The cobles of Craster

The wooded street of Lesbury

The lobster pots of Boulmer

Rock: an estate village

Was Duns Scotus born at Dunstan Hall?

Wark-
worth and
its castle

Northumberland he would "burn a tower of mine within three miles of my poor house at Warkworth, where I lie, and give me light to put on my clothes at midnight." When the time came, however, having "no flint and fizzle" with him, Ker murdered a pregnant woman and took himself off again.

The derivation of the name Warkworth is shrouded in mystery. One explanation is that it was a Worth, or Homestead, belonging to Wearca, a seventh-century abbess of Tynemouth; another that it was the Homestead where there was an abundance of Spiders; or perhaps the place was named after a Weaver, or a Wayfarer, or even after someone nicknamed the Spider!

If you have any choice, approach the village from the north. That way you not only get full value from the lovely old bridge over the Coquet, but you see the village as it should be seen, that is to say with the castle in the background—an unforgettable picture. Even then it is not possible to appreciate the extraordinary lay-out of the place, and only a glance at the map really shows how it grew up inside a horseshoe bend in the Coquet—the open end being sealed, as it were by the hill on which is built that "worm-eaten hold of ragged stone" that is the castle.

It is not long since the only way across the river was by way of the sole fortified bridge in the north (and one of only a few in England) which was built in the fourteenth century, and subsequently widened. Its tower now lacks a parapet, but is otherwise complete, with its arched opening into a porter's lodge, and corkscrew staircase to an upper floor. An outer defence to the castle, which has no curtain wall on this side, but only a moat, the tower was once a defensive necessity; but with its archway just wide enough and high enough for a single motor car to pass through, it has proved something of a problem in the twentieth century. It was obviously out of the question to take it down, so, however distasteful it must have been, another bridge had to be built alongside.

Close by is Bridge End House, built early in the eighteenth century, with moulded window-frames and contemporary iron gate and railings. Along a little tree-lined street that follows the river eastwards, stands the Borough School, a plain-looking cottage with red-tiled roof and the date 1736. Here the schoolmaster lived on the upper floor and taught in the rooms below. In the early

M

days of this century it was used for vestry and ratepayers' meetings but it is now falling into disrepair.

Near the bridge, also, is a magnificent church dedicated to St Lawrence—a rarity in that it is almost pure Norman. Like Norham, it is more like a young cathedral inside than a parish church; an impression enhanced by its resemblance to Durham.

If the church has altered little throughout the ages, so, in its general conformation, has the village. With its saltpans and all the trade that the castle inspired, Warkworth has always been a flourishing place, and no less so now that it attracts so many tourists. The houses, of dressed stone, have probably been rebuilt several times, but the shape of the village remains that of the borough laid out in the twelfth century, with a wide street leading up from the bridge to the castle, and the gardens sloping down to the river, much as the original crofts did. The burgesses even retain the right (except where they have sold it to the Lord of the Manor) to pasture their cattle on the 'stints', or half-acre plots, on the common land south-west of the village, and some of the houses still retain the passage-ways through which the cows were driven in to be milked. Only the cherished right of the villagers to make middens in the street seems to have been curtailed.

The great glory of Warkworth is, of course, the castle on its hill overlooking the Coquet, with its lovely Norman keep. Built, most probably, by that Earl of Northumberland who was a son of David I of Scotland, and wrested from him by Henry I, its recapture by the Scots resulted in the wretched villagers who had taken refuge in the 'minster' of St Lawrence being dragged out and slaughtered. Rebuilt by the Claverings, Lords of Warkworth, and besieged without success by Robert Bruce, the castle was awarded by Edward III with the rest of the Clavering estates to Henry Percy, Lord of Alnwick—its original owner, Henry the Strong, being succeeded by Henry the Short, who was followed by Henry, the first Earl of the Percy line and victor of Homildon Hill.

It was Warkworth that Shakespeare immortalized in *Henry IV*, for here in the castle Northumberland and his son Harry Hotspur hatched the plot which was to embroil so many of the great magnates in rebellion. After the death of Hotspur at the battle of Shrewsbury, and the imprisonment of his father, Hotspur's son,

Sir Henry Percy, refused to surrender the castle, and managed, though he could not have been more than fourteen at the time, to hold on until his grandfather was released. Overawed, however, by the enormous cannon that the king brought against the castle, grandfather and grandson finally decided that discretion was the better part of valour. They departed hurriedly to Scotland and the castle capitulated.

In the Wars of the Roses both the second and third Earls of Northumberland died for the Lancastrian cause, and the castle passed into the hands of that same Duke of Clarence who was eventually upended in a butt of Malmsey wine. Eventually it was returned to the Percys. Henry the Magnificent (the fifth Earl) hardly used the place, but his son, Henry the Unthrifty, lived there a good deal.

It was the Gunpowder Plot that really spelt the end of the castle, for the current Earl found himself in the Tower as a result, the place was let and allowed to fall into a disgraceful state of dis-repair. When the Earl was released, he relet it to Sir Francis Brandling who surrendered it (he was a Royalist) to the Scots in 1644. Four years later Cromwell placed a garrison in the castle, and when they left, they were told "to take away all doors to be kept in safety, for preventing a sudden holding by any second taking; but for walls, iron or other materials they were not to meddle with." Instead, the garrison demolished everything they could, which was tough on the Earl, himself a Parliamentarian.

And so the deterioration continued until the castle suffered the usual fate of such places, and became a quarry for the use of anyone who cared to despoil it—in this case the administrators of the estate itself. Now it is in the hands of the Department of the Environment, and a splendid job they make of it.

It is a happy accident that a book about a county famous for its castles and for its Border legends should end with a little of each, for one only has to row a mile or so up the river in a boat provided for the purpose to come upon the finest hermitage in England, in the shape of a cell and chapel carved out of the solid rock of the river bank. With it goes an equally romantic legend about Sir Bertram of Bothal who loved the beautiful daughter of Lord Widdrington. On her way to make her peace with her lover, whom she regretted having dared to join an expedition against the Scots, she herself was captured by the enemy, but escaped down a rope with the help of her brother. Thinking that the latter was some unknown rival, Bertram achieved a most unfortunate right-and-left by stabbing her brother and, in the process, the fair Isabel as well. As a penance, he is supposed to have carved out the hermitage, in which he spent the rest of his life. So runs the legend. The truth is less romantic, for in reality the first of a line of hermits appointed by the fourth Earl was one Thomas Barker. No one seems to know whether it was he who did the carving, but it is a monumental work, with a living-room and kitchen on the ground floor, and a vaulted chapel above, some twenty feet long, and approached through a tiny porch with a stone seat on either side.

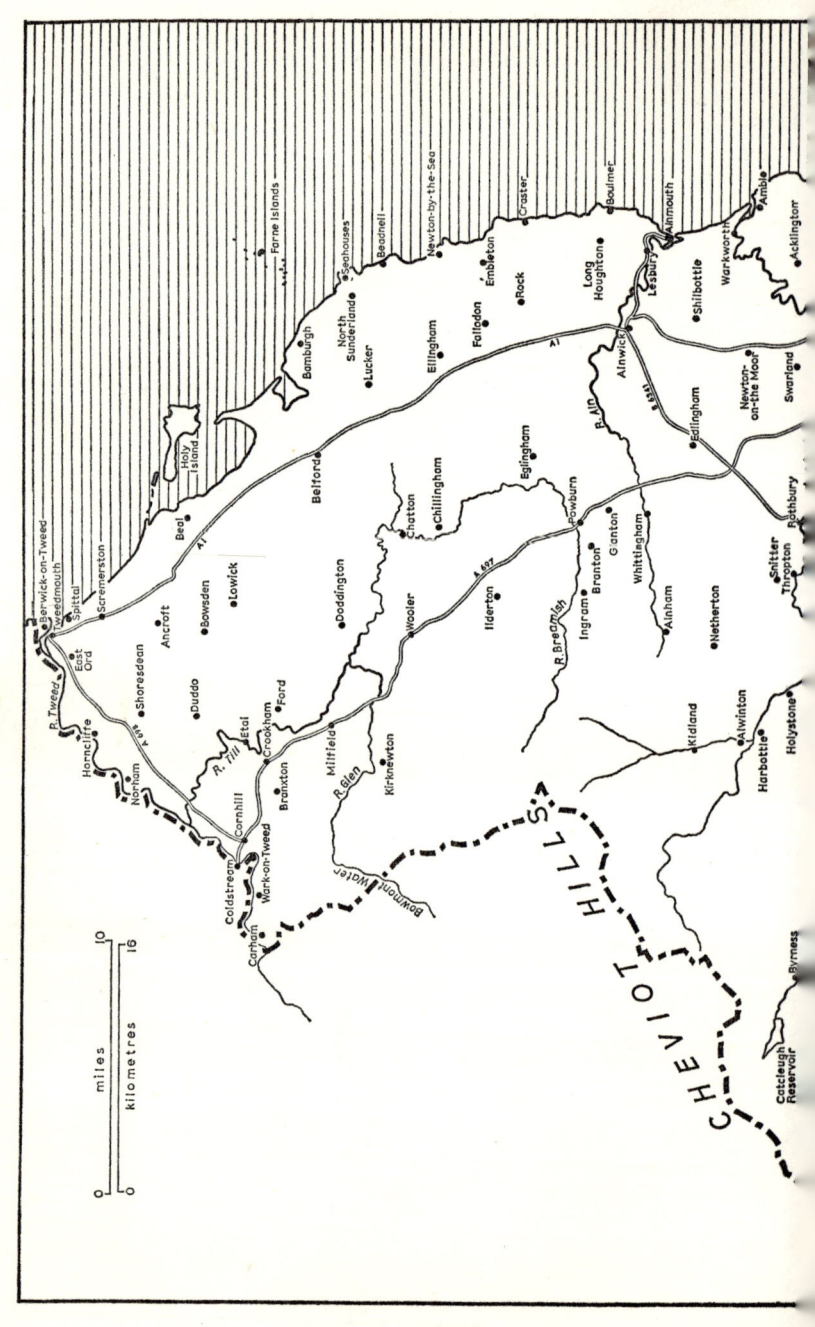

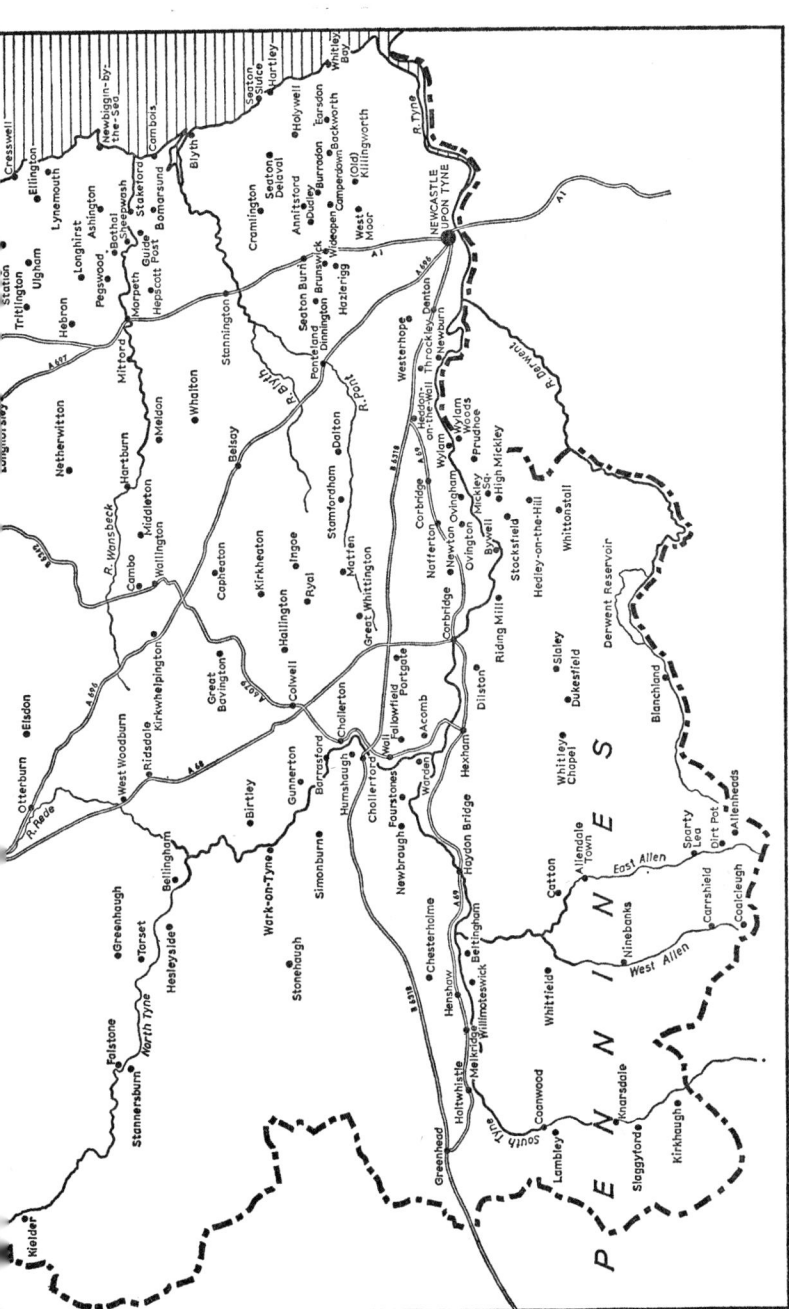

(Based with permission on the Ordnance Survey)

Index